T0271756

The No Worries Guide to Raising Your Anxious Child

of related interest

How to Have Incredible Conversations with your Child
A Collaborative Workbook for Parents, Carers and Children
to Encourage Meaningful Communication
Jane Gilmour and Bettina Hohnen
ISBN 978 1 78775 640 3
eISBN 978 1 78775 641 0

The Incredible Teenage Brain
Everything You Need to Know to Unlock Your Teen's Potential
Bettina Hohnen, Jane Gilmour and Tara Murphy
Illustrated by Douglas Broadley
Foreword by Sarah Jayne Blakemore
ISBN 978 1 78592 557 3
eISBN 978 1 78450 952 1

Teen Mental Health in an Online World
Supporting Young People around their Use of Social
Media, Apps, Gaming, Texting and the Rest
Victoria Betton and James Woollard
ISBN 978 1 78592 468 2
eISBN 978 1 78450 852 4

Starving the Anxiety Gremlin
A Cognitive Behavioural Therapy Workbook on
Anxiety Management for Young People
Kate Collins-Donnelly
ISBN 978 1 84905 341 9
eISBN 978 0 85700 673 8

My Anxiety Handbook
Getting Back on Track
Sue Knowles, Bridie Gallagher and Phoebe McEwen
Illustrated by Emmeline Pidgen
ISBN 978 1 78592 440 8
eISBN 978 1 78450 813 5

The No Worries Guide to Raising Your Anxious Child

A Handbook to Help You and Your Anxious Child Thrive

Karen Lynn Cassiday, PhD, ACT

Jessica Kingsley Publishers
London and Philadelphia

First published in Great Britain in 2022 by Jessica Kingsley Publishers
An Hachette Company

1

A CIP catalogue record for this title is available from
the British Library and the Library of Congress

ISBN 978 1 78775 887 2
eISBN 978 1 78775 888 9

Printed and bound by CPI Group (UK) Ltd, Croydon, CR0 4YY

Jessica Kingsley Publishers' policy is to use papers that are natural,
renewable and recyclable products and made from wood grown in
sustainable forests. The logging and manufacturing processes are expected
to conform to the environmental regulations of the country of origin.

Jessica Kingsley Publishers
Carmelite House
50 Victoria Embankment
London EC4Y 0DZ

www.jkp.com

Contents

Author's Note: For the sake of convenience, I will refer to all offspring, ages one through young adult, as children and use the gender-neutral pronouns them, they and their to respect the variety of ages, developmental stages and expressions of gender reflected in all children.

Trigger Warning: This book mentions content that might be upsetting to readers who have emetophobia (fear of vomiting), anxiety about illness, medical procedures or medical instruments, distress about the mention of dying and death, difficulty with pregnancy, distress about the mention of disability and distress about the mention of mental illness.

CHAPTER 1

Accidentally Getting the Short Stick in the Game of Parenting

Have you ever secretly watched families with disabled kids, misbehaving kids or kids with mental illness and pitied them, or felt sorry for them? When you thought about the parents of these families, have you ever elevated the status of the parents to heroic "Aren't they amazing! Look at what they do with such a difficult situation?" or secretly thought a few judgmental thoughts such as "Wonder what went wrong in that family that their kid ended up being so anxious?" or "Their kids wouldn't be so out of control if the parents would just follow through with good discipline or get therapy." When you were observing those families, it probably never occurred to you that you might end up being one of "those" parents, the parents who have the challenge of trying to figure out how to raise a kid whose upbringing is destined to be different no matter what. You might even secretly have the thought that even though you adore your child, you really feel overwhelmed when your child's anxiety makes the day really difficult, really grueling and like something that feels like drawing the short stick in the game of parenting.

There are many things that parents like to avoid thinking about and talking about when it comes to the topic of raising an anxious child. No one likes to talk about the fact that if you have a child with any mental health challenge, your own mental health and physical health are at risk. Parents of children with any type of disability, such as attention deficit hyperactivity disorder (ADHD), developmental delays, or any mental illness, are more likely to die an average of ten years younger than mothers of normally developing children, and the parents of kids with any of these challenges have a 20 up to 80 percent risk of divorce (Grcevich, 2016). Eighty percent of parents of children with mental health disorders or disabilities are likely to suffer from anxiety disorders and depression (Scherer, Verhey & Kuper, 2019). If your child or teen requires lots of intervention, then you are at an even greater risk simply because it is more difficult to take vacations, get adequate sleep or to spend relaxed time with friends or family. Additionally, no one likes to mention the fact that the younger your child is when they first show symptoms of anxiety then the more likely they are to need repeated intervention and to develop other mental health disorders throughout their lifetime. This is why so many of the parents of my young patients look at me with dismay when I talk about their likely need to return to treatment even though they just successfully completed a course of treatment. Being the parent of an anxious child is likely going to be an ongoing challenge no matter how well you do your part.

As I write these facts, I think back to what happened to me as I careened back and forth between being totally smitten and in love with my firstborn and being totally undone by things that were not like what other parents experienced. I did my best to put on a brave face, just in the same way that I see the parents of my patients put on a brave face. I was too terrified to face my worries about what might be ahead for my child and my family. I was a mental health professional who knew too much and a mother who wanted to hope for the best. I was lost. What I most wanted to know was whether or not there was anything that I could do to help my child grow into a competent, kind and useful adult. I had flocks of therapists and doctors who were all focused on single components of my child's development but none of whom could tell me what to do about developing my child's resilience, character and self-worth in a life that I knew would be challenging from the beginning. What good is being able to walk and talk if other people are put off by my son running away each time he feels shy around other kids? Being really bright might be nice, but if your child is unwilling to participate in any activities other than video games and schoolwork, then being bright is not of much use.

The problem I faced is common to parents of all children who require therapists, doctors, special education and other specialists. Many professionals make the assumption that if your child or teen can overcome their symptoms then they will live good and full lives. This was the assumption I had as a young newly minted psychologist. It is the assumption that I see the parents of my patients make. I was incorrect.

The burgeoning field of positive psychology has shown that there are separate skills of mental wellness that lead to resilience and strong self-worth. Resilience is your ability to persevere under duress while remaining hopeful for a better future. Self-worth is what you feel when you know there is a small gap between who you know you are in your character and who you wish you could be. Self-worth is a measure of moral integrity that guides us to be better people and to take pride in the virtues of being human. Self-esteem, on the other hand, is who you are based upon your accomplishments. Self-esteem is shallow and does not lead to a deep sense of integrity and self-satisfaction because it is dependent upon circumstance. People who are resilient, or gritty, and who have a deep abiding sense of self-worth based upon good character are the true winners in life. They experience joy, purpose and success at work and in relationships regardless of their circumstances, public successes or limitations. They thrive on their empathy and generosity toward others and develop the ability to take care of their own emotional needs as well as care for others. If I want anything for my children and my patients, it is to develop these qualities. These qualities will give them a big advantage in living a life that has more challenges than the average person.

The problem, therefore, is what can you do to become the type of parent who sets the stage for your child who already has the challenge of anxiety? If you are reading this book, chances are that you are already asking yourself how you can make something beautiful out of something messy and unexpected. You might be grieving the very fact of your child's diagnosis, or diagnoses, or be feeling resentful at the unfairness of it all. You will have to start with cultivating your own resilience and reshaping your expectations so you can parent your child according to who they are, instead of according to who others think they should be. You will have to learn to laugh at your own foolishness and the absurdity of your family's life. You will have to learn to embrace your child's anxiety as an opportunity for growth instead of mourning the loss of who you hoped your child would be.

You will have to overcome your deep desire to make things right by accidentally making life too easy for your child and accidentally accommodating your child's anxiety. You will need to cultivate joy every day, so you show your child how to find their joy in the middle of challenge and fear.

I am telling you the secret that all good child therapists know. When you change for the better, you help your child change for the better. This book will be your two-for-one guidebook to help both you and your child learn to live a life of joy in which your worry and your child's anxiety take a back seat. This book will teach you the proven scientific steps that are powerful, positive and practical and that will help you and your family thrive no matter what.

What the books and blogs don't tell you when you get pregnant

I remember the first time I cracked open the cover of *What to Expect When You Are Expecting* (Murkoff, 2016). It felt like I was opening the gate to a wonderful and very adult initiation into the world of parenthood. I had imagined being a parent my entire life. I had watched other women have children and overheard the conversations of the grownups talking about their children. Like many would-be parents, I had loved babysitting kids, being a camp counselor and Girl Scout leader and had trained in graduate school to provide therapy to children. The truth is, I felt really prepared and totally enthusiastic about getting pregnant and becoming a mother. Here is the part in this book where you need to imagine hearing that weird scratchy TV sitcom sound that indicates something is about to go really wrong.

I also prided myself on being this really organized together sort of person who could manage my professional career as a clinical psychologist, my social life, my weight, my health and my schedule. If you aren't already guffawing at my hubris and naivete you should be. Here is what I got. It took much longer than I had expected to get pregnant. It took until my husband had to get that test for sperm motility before his little wigglers made successful contact with my eggs. I had a high risk pregnancy that started with vomiting all day long, having three episodes of bedrest due to the placenta partially separating from my uterus, severe reflux due to severe vomiting, then repeated bouts of pneumonia due to all of the vomiting followed by broken ribs caused by severe coughing that had been caused by severe vomiting. I also spent three months of my pregnancy on bedrest taking all kinds of drugs that the textbooks said were bad for my baby's development. My doctor told me afterwards that my pregnancy was so alarming that he advised me to never get pregnant again. In hindsight, I did not appreciate that this experience of life out of control was a great predictor for my experience of parenthood. Sometimes you get what you imagined but most of the time in parenthood you end up in situations and emotional states that you never imagined. Playing Rock, Paper, Scissors to see who gets to change the next diaper? Check. Learning that your child needs emergency psychiatric hospitalization? Check. Giving your older teen the finger behind their back when in an anxious rage they tell you how you and all other adults have permanently ruined the entire world? Check.

No one likes to admit that parenting is the one job that is guaranteed to make us grow up fast and challenge our unrealistic hopes of being the ideal parent we imagined for ourselves and our partner, when we have one. No one likes to openly speak of what it means to raise a child who does not develop typically for fear of sounding pitiable or self-pitying. When you look at the research on life stressors, the only thing worse than having a child die is giving birth to a child (Noone, 2017). Also, the thing most likely to decrease your marital satisfaction is having a baby and this effect lasts at least three years. The study ended after three years, but, based on my professional and personal experience, I would be willing to bet all my future earnings that things get even worse during the preteen and teen years.

No matter who you give birth to, they will not be what you expected, especially if your child has an anxiety disorder. They will be human. They will be complicated. They will be both wonderful and frustrating. They will not be like all the things that you imagined before the baby arrived. They will fuss, cry, be avoidant of things that most children enjoy or tantrum at the most awkward moments, like when the neighbor kid catches a spider in a jar and brings it over to show off. Likewise, you will not be what you expected. You will be human. You will be complicated. You will have to learn to rise to greatness in the middle of your own worry. You will have to learn to recover from your own humanity and that of your children's and your partner's. In short, you will be thoroughly human despite all your love and good intentions. You will fail just as many times as you succeed. This means that if you really want to get into the business of being a parent, especially the parent of a child with anxiety, you had better take a detailed look at your expectations, even if you think they are realistic. Failure to reset your expectations will set you and your family up for unnecessary heartache and failure. So, rule number one in not going crazy and accidentally making things worse for yourself and your anxious child is to embrace your humanity and your child's anxious version of humanity.

PARENT RESILIENCY RULE 1

Learn to embrace your humanity and your child's humanity.

The parents I work with who raise anxious children get tangled in the desire to be heroic and somehow return their child's life to normal. They accidentally engage in accommodation behaviors designed to alleviate anxiety and make things easier in the moment when it is precisely the wrong moment to make things easy. I, too, really wanted to believe that my parenting might prevent problems in my children's behavior, especially in public and at school. I sincerely believed that if I did my job right at home by insisting on polite behaviors, being a good example, noticing and praising my children's politeness and talking to them about the value of respectful polite behavior from the time of birth, then they would most certainly be polite, even with disabilities or mental health conditions. I completely overlooked the fact that my children were typical human beings who could be influenced by my parenting but not totally controlled. I forgot to take into account two factors, what I had been like as a child when I was tired, irritable, hungry, anxious or otherwise not at my best, and what effect anxiety and depression might have upon my child's ability to cope. I forgot that my dad used to keep a poster on the back on his workroom door in the basement that had a picture of an ape that looked crazed and said, "Someday I hope my child gets to raise a child just like you!" I forgot the experience of my patients in which a seemingly small event could result in hours rather than minutes of tantrums. I forgot to let go of my ideal image of my child and family.

I also bought into all the hype in the parenting books and magazine articles and the talk amongst my friends and other parents that suggested that any really competent parent would never have one of "those" kids. "Those" kids meant one of those kids who threw the foam blocks in the play area, one of those kids who refused to talk to anyone in preschool, one of those kids who refused to ask for help and would rather fail a test because it was too embarrassing to raise their hand in class, or one of those kids who used all of their lunch tickets to buy all the lunch cookies thereby creating a cookie monopoly in which they then resold them at great profit to the kids who had pocket money so they could be popular. "Those" kids meant the kids who need special education and therapists and special medications. "Those" kids were my kids.

I absorbed the message that you and other parents hear everywhere. If you do your job right, then your kids will make you proud. If you put in your time as a parent, then your family will be wonderful. If you do your best work, then your child will overcome their limitations. No one was talking about what it meant to raise one of "those" kids who were less likely to look like the kids everyone admires and desires.

My pre-pregnancy expectations were based on an edited version of my past in which I recalled my proud moments and the fun moments that comprised my family's history. I recalled the way my great aunts threw book-themed birthday parties that were magical. I imagined having several daughters who were like the film-worthy version of my childhood. I forgot that no matter what sort of parent I was or what sort of kid I had, my kids were going to do all kinds of private and public things that would make me quickly decide that I had two choices, die in shame or become the sort of parent who couldn't be shamed. My experience as a therapist showed me that I had better choose becoming impervious to shame.

What I did remember was how others would get hushed when they talked about the parents of kids who had mental health conditions and how everyone kept it a secret if a child or teen in the family went to a psychiatric hospital. I vowed that if I had kids who fit into these categories then I would proudly display my kids in public just like all of the other moms. I would never fall victim to shame! What I didn't take into account was how painful it feels when you realize that, despite your best intentions, the messages from the current parenting culture about "those kids" still exist inside yourself and in others. We are all easy prey for unhelpful cultural ideals for parents and their children. It looks so good on film and social media. It seems so charming and desirable when you see someone else's child succeed in a seemingly effortless way and do all the things that appear to be so perfect.

The problem with shame

Shame has become the predominant inner world that parents feel when their kid acts human or doesn't quite meet the expectations of others. Media and unhealthy cultural norms now tell us that we are supposed to make sure that our kids never do things that are embarrassing, annoying or immoral, even when they have conditions that might make this especially challenging. We are supposed to raise kids who evoke the admiration of others. We are supposed to be able to post admirable things about our children on social media, or at least entertaining things. No one says it quite like that. Instead they say things that act like this is true. For example, a group of parents is sitting around the ball pit and someone else's kid happens to get a little overexcited and begins to throw balls. One of the balls hits an infant's face and the infant begins to cry. What typically happens next is the following: A bunch of parents frown at the kid who threw the ball and rush to protect their kids. They also frown at the parents of the ball thrower. The parent of the crying kid glares at the kid who threw the ball and begins to worry about potential head injury. They likely scold the embarrassed parents of the kid who threw the ball. Several other parents try to get their kids to play away from the kid who threw the ball because they now misperceive this kid as dangerous. They mutter about how the ball thrower should not be permitted in the ball pit because he throws balls. They probably text other parents about how there is a really bad and dangerous kid who is now ruining the safety of the ball pit for everyone. The parents of the budding baseball pitcher try to apologize to the parents of the crying baby and tell their child not to throw balls. The parents of the budding baseball pitcher are so flustered by everyone's disapproval they forget to tell their kid to apologize because they know that their child is now viewed as the Godzilla of the ball pit. The parents who now fear that the ball-throwing kid is dangerous will likely go tell the manager that this dangerous child needs to be told to leave the play area. Or they might just leave early to prevent potential injury to their child.

What did this scene just teach all of the kids? Making a mistake earns community disapproval and terrible shame. Mistakes cannot be undone or recovered from. Crying or feeling momentarily scared is very bad and should be avoided at all costs. Bumps and bruises are not permissible during normal play. Accidentally hurting or scaring others is bad and ruins everything. The parent is a failure for having a kid who does something that looks like fun and made another child cry.

What did this teach all of the parents? Watch your kid like a hawk because they are in danger of either being hurt or of hurting another kid. Shame is to be avoided at all costs, so you better closely monitor your kid for any sign of behavior that seems a bit too high spirited or spontaneous. If your kid cries it is terrible. If your kid makes another kid cry it is grounds for public shaming. Apologies are ineffective. A kid who throws balls is an embarrassment. It is better to avoid ball pits.

If you happen to have a kid who is more likely to do those sorts of things that bring about public shaming, then you are under even more pressure to get it right. Having a kid with anxiety that makes them more impulsive, more avoidant, more compulsive or less like perfect can make life feel like a minefield of shame unless you learn a different way to think and act.

What is wrong with this scenario? First, way too many parents are focusing upon crafting their idealized version of play and think of play's sole purpose as creating a happy experience. The purpose of play is not to create happiness. It is to create mastery. Good play involves risk taking, testing the limits, making and recovering from mistakes and recovering from accidents. Play is the work of childhood that prepares the child to become an adult. Play involves many things besides having fun. That includes throwing balls that sometimes bounce off another child's head. Take play wrestling as an example. We know that children who play wrestle with their parents are likely to have better social skills and less social anxiety than kids who do not (Borchard, 2018; Schiffrin *et al.*, 2015). Why? The give and take of play wrestling, sometimes getting hurt and sometimes discovering how you can hurt someone, teaches you how to read nonverbal social cues and how to exhibit self-control while having fun. Play wrestling teaches kids how to define the fine line between what someone else experiences as fun versus being too much. Kids also learn when to give in and let others win versus when to continue to wrestle and win. Children who engage in rough and tumble play also develop better social skills and are perceived as more likeable by other children (Borchard, 2018). The same is true for kids who are allowed to climb playground equipment, ride bikes, climb trees and more. Kids need to learn the limits of their bodies, their imagination, their emotions and their friendships by doing things until they get it right, including the kids who have more difficulty learning these skills. That also means it is necessary and beneficial to do things wrong so you can learn from it.

This necessitates play that is not ruled by parents. If you want your kid to grow, then you need to hope that they throw a few balls and get hit by a few balls. You need to let them fall, get scrapes, get stuck and then get unstuck without your help. This is especially true for kids whose anxiety limits their play. For example, your child might take longer to warm up and play with others, might be scared when the balls start flying through the air or might get worried about how untidy everything is in the ball pit. The truth is that the balls in the ball pit are not dangerous. Crying is not dangerous and making a mistake is ordinary and always forgivable. Why shouldn't a kid be allowed to throw the balls in a ball pit? Aren't balls for throwing anyway? Entertaining the expectation that any child will be able to engage in any play without having conflict, bumps and misunderstandings is unrealistic. If you want your child to grow, then you want them to be testing the limits of play and of other kids and grownups so they learn who they are and how things work. The truth is that practice makes perfect. Kids who have limitations imposed on their development or mental health need the same amount and type of practice as all kids do. The mistake that many parents of anxious kids make is to limit these opportunities because they fear the shame of what happens when something does not go to plan, especially for their anxious child whom they may misperceive as being more vulnerable and needing more parental assistance to avoid emotional pain.

A second problem with this scenario is that parents are accidentally assuming that things going wrong is somehow dangerous. They assume that it is emotionally dangerous for a child to experience the surprise of a head bump and the experience of crying. It may be unpleasant to be surprised, to get bumped or to get bruised, but it is not dangerous. Every child needs to learn how to bounce back from unpleasant surprise, frustration and momentary pain, especially kids whose anxiety makes them worry about such things happening. For example, one of my sons, who had selective mutism and social anxiety disorder, always wanted to avoid all group activities and worried on the way to every activity that he would get hurt or embarrassed, no matter how much fun he ended up having once he got involved. He did this from birth until age seventeen. His anxiety made him imagine the worst-case scenario for every sport, activity or game no matter his skill level and no matter how much fun he had the last time he did the activity. For example, at age three, he cried before the first half season of football practices, telling me "What if I kick it wrong? What if I fall over? What if I don't know what to do?" It was difficult dragging a crying child onto the playing field while acting calm and like this was no big deal, but I did it because I knew that it was supremely important that my son learn that his fear was inaccurate and nothing to listen to.

I wanted him to learn to push past his fear and discover his inner strength even as a three-year-old. I knew that I did not want to delay helping him develop good mental health by giving in to his fear and desire to avoid feeling embarrassed.

These experiences are inevitable. Young children should get enough practice at doing things that scare them, seem frustrating or tedious so that it is no big deal to feel anxious, frustrated, challenged or momentarily defeated by the time they are teens or young adults. Part of learning to live comfortably with other humans is to learn that accidental harm and embarrassment may come your way and it is no big deal. We all need to learn that we are never entitled to have life go the way we expect it to go. Whether it is having our toes stepped upon, another driver zipping into our lane at high speed or our neighbor having a loud party when we want to sleep, we need to learn to be tolerant and forgiving if we want to maintain good mental health. The development of the ability to be tolerant and forgiving starts in infancy and early childhood.

The only way to learn tolerance and forgiveness is through practice. We learn to be tolerant by repeatedly experiencing inconvenience and discomfort while resisting the urge to complain and act entitled. We have to change our expectation away from one of entitlement to a life of comfort and convenience for ourselves and our child, and instead gracefully accept that most of life involves lots of discomfort and inconvenience. This is the secret advantage of your child's anxiety disorder. It is a chance to repeatedly practice courage, persistence and patience. It is one reason my oldest son with cerebral palsy is so upbeat and uncomplaining when he falls, trips or gets scrapes and cuts. He is used to it because it has happened every day of his life and he has accepted that it is the price of self-ambulation and independence.

A third problem with the ball pit scenario is that parents are accidentally assuming that their kids are well behaved for not throwing the ball and that the virtuous parents are the ones with kids who did not throw balls. They were just lucky at that moment. If your kid is developing normally and especially if they are athletically inclined, they are at high risk of wanting to throw, climb and otherwise test out the properties of their body and anything that can be moved. This is why kids like playgrounds in the first place. If your child is not athletically inclined, then they need to be encouraged to do things like throw the ball and jump in the ball pit so they discover that they, too, can have fun in their body. If a kid is not testing the limits of the ball pit or waiting for permission from their mother to play, then something is wrong. When your child takes risks, they are growing in mastery of their body, emotions and the environment. If you have a child whose anxiety disorder makes risk taking difficult, then they need lots of encouragement and permission to play with vigor. That is why we forced our aforementioned son to attend so many group activities, because we knew that, at some point, he would learn he could take on any challenge, even when he did not feel up to it. Just to prove that this worked, last year this same son entered himself in a military "Rucksmarch" that involved running for several hours over hilly terrain while carrying a 30-kilogram backpack and wearing Army boots. He openly admitted that he was scared to death that he might not finish, but he trained two months for the event and completed it in the middle of the pack!

A fourth problem is that many parents mistake crying as being undesirable. They take the stance that anything done to their child that causes crying must be bad and worth disapproval. This is profoundly unhelpful. While it is never fun to hear your child cry, it is inevitable. Crying is the only way for an infant to communicate during the early months until smiling emerges and the infant begins to develop voluntary facial expressions. Most adults only cry when there is extreme emotion, such as joy, grief, anger or great mirth. They forget that children, teens and emerging adults cry more readily and more frequently due to their developmentally normal emotional immaturity. Parents can forget that crying is not harmful for a child to experience. In a toddler or child or teen, it is simply a signal that stronger emotions are present and self-management skills are under development.

HOT TIP

Remind yourself that crying is simply a signal that emotions are present and self-management skills are under development.

The truth is that your kid and *all* kids get into trouble, make mistakes, do foolish things and take a long time to become people we admire. It is much easier to avoid feeling ashamed, alarmed and overwhelmed about your child's limitations when you realize that every moment is just another learning opportunity for your child. You do not have to rush when something goes wrong. No matter what you do, your child will still take a long time to grow up. If you can take the perspective that lots of time and repeated practice are the necessary ingredients for your child to grow up, then you can take away the pressure to get it right the first time.

HOT TIP

If you take the perspective that it is normal and necessary for your kid to need lots of practice to grow up,
including learning how to manage their anxiety, you
will take away the pressure to have your kid get it right
the first, second or third time.

A fifth problem is that kids learn best by doing. We all do. The
idea that having a talk, reading a book to a child about good
manners, or attending a special assembly will teach a child how
to handle the rough and tumble of life is absurd. Kids learn
by doing and by observing what happens when other people
do things. What you say is much less powerful than how you
act. Trying out different behaviors to see what happens is the
normal process for human development. Even though your
kid might talk a lot and ask many questions, they are still using
their daily experience as their primary means of learning. This
is why our warnings, heart to heart talks and approval can only
go so far. Most kids are going to have to do some deliberate
breaking of the rules in order to learn the rules. Kids with
anxiety disorders are likely going to do annoying things when
they are feeling anxious. Many of the parents I see are shocked
or worried about the severity of oppositional behaviors their
anxious child exhibits. They fear that it indicates that something more than anxiety is terribly wrong or that there has
been a catastrophic breakdown in their relationship with their
child. Anxiety causes the fight, flight or freeze response, which
translates into crying fits, yelling, running away, refusing to
get out of bed, avoiding school or other unpleasant behaviors. It's why your normally polite and rule-following child

can become a rude, nasty and inconsiderate beast when they have an anxiety attack. There is no shame in this. There is no parent who can overcome this process with the right cuddle and special talk. This is just the normal experience of a child who is overwhelmed by anxiety and lacks the skills necessary to manage themselves in a constructive way.

So, here is what I believe would be the ideal healthy redo for the scene in the ball pit. Parents sit around, enjoying each other and enjoying their kids playing in the ball pit. A kid throws a ball that bonks another child in the head and this child begins to cry. The nearest parent reassures the crying child that it must have been a surprise to get bonked and no wonder they are crying. They tell the crying child that the child will be OK, that no damage has been done and return to the other parents once the child shows signs of calming down. The parent of the kid who threw the ball tells their child in a calm friendly voice, "Let's try not to throw balls at the other kids. Looks like you will have to work on your aim. Throw them over here instead. Let's go apologize to the child who is crying and say that you are sorry you scared them and made them cry." The other parents continue to let their children play and tell both the ball thrower's parents and the bonked child's parents, "Been there, done that. My children had the same thing happen. Most children get overexcited in the ball pit and throw balls that hit someone or accidentally kick another child while they are squirming," and "Your child will get over it. Surprises can be scary when you are young. Look they are playing again and back to having fun."

What does this alternate scenario teach all the parents and children? Accidents happen even when you are having fun. These accidents are no big deal and the fun can continue. You take responsibility and apologize even when you accidentally hurt someone or scare someone. You can handle upset whether you are a parent or a child. Other parents have your back and support you when your child acts like a child. Making mistakes is no big deal, just an opportunity to learn and grow. There is no shame in being a parent or in being a child. Wouldn't it be wonderful if you felt this way and others acted this way whenever kids played together?

My children made me get a lot of practice at refining my sense of what really constituted a catastrophe and made me uproot a lot of pointless shame. I truly had never thought of the possibility that I might be the parent who would have to learn to manage the following situations:

Awkward Mom Moment 1: Going to my first parent teacher conference with the glowing memory of loving these meetings with my teachers and parents because my teacher always talked about how much she enjoyed having me in her class, pointed out the exceptional things that I did and reassured my parents about things I did not do so well at, like handwriting and spelling. It was a mutual admiration glowy sort of experience. Here is what typically happened with my son. I waited outside the teacher's classroom while I overheard several of these glowy conversations about the students ahead of my son. I walked in and noticed that the teacher did not make immediate eye contact and spent a lot of time looking at her papers. The teacher mentioned the lovely color of my son's auburn hair and then told us that she was concerned about whether or not my son was learning enough and wanted to know if he had any friends at school because he would always run away when the other kids greeted him. She asked me and his father "What should be done about that?" I also looked up at the bulletin board where my son proudly pointed out the one art project that looked like an elephant stepped in finger paint and walked across the paper. All of the other paintings looked like things I could recognize. My inner dialogue went something like this: "Wait, why is she only saying nice things about his hair? My son loves school. Hasn't he learned more than this? I have been reading with him every night since he seemed like his eyes could focus on me. I thought he had friends because he talks about what he and the other kids do. OMG! That painting sure looks like my son did it. Do other kindergarteners really paint that well? Why is the teacher asking us what to do? Isn't she supposed to tell us? I am a psychologist, not a teacher!" Then fill in the blank with your preferred expletives because that is where my mind went at this point in the conference.

Awkward Mom Moment 2: I rushed to the grocery store during rush hour in the hope that I could get all the things I forgot to get over the weekend due to being so busy with managing my toddler pulling anything out of the cabinets and getting lost in the house by log rolling under beds and sofas. I raced around the store grabbing groceries and gave my son the car keys to play with so I could shop. This worked really well, until we got into the checkout line. I then gave him my debit card in addition to car keys to hold since that caught his attention, would occupy both hands and decreased the likelihood of him grabbing things. This worked really well while I transferred groceries from the cart to the conveyor belt. Then the grocery conveyor belt made a weird screeching noise and came to a halt. The checkout guy looked at me and said, "Ma'am, your debit card and car keys are jamming the mechanism on the conveyor." He then proceeded to use the store intercom to announce to everyone, "Lady's car keys and debit card jamming the conveyor on register number eight. Engineer needed to fix conveyor on register number eight." After what seemed like forever, the engineer arrived and announced to everyone, "I have never had this happen before!" By then, the line of shoppers behind me were abandoning my checkout line. A crowd of spectators gathered when the engineer pulled all the metal housing off the conveyor belt and dragged out his large canvas tool bag. My son, on the other hand, thought this whole procedure was fascinating and strained to get out of the shopping cart seat. He said in a very loud and excited voice "Momma, momma, momma. Lemme see. Lemme see!" It took the next twenty minutes for the engineer to fix the conveyor belt and get my keys and debit card unstuck. Throughout the entire process my son was making loud enthusiastic commentary and asking loud toddler questions, "Why did he do that? Why did it get stuck? What is he gonna do?"

Awkward Mom Moment 3: My youngest son found all costumed characters and clowns to be terrifying. We took him to an annual cross-country ski marathon in which they had a children's short race that he could compete in for the first time. We were so excited because he was so excited and not giving us the usual protests about participating, likely because the parents walked alongside the preschoolers as they skied. Unfortunately, as we were on our way to the starting line, we saw a large group of clowns who were entertaining the children and also wearing skis. My son began crying loudly and hid behind me and then announced that he no longer wanted to ski because of "mean clowns." I had to pick him up and tote him under one arm while I held my ski poles and pretended it was no big deal that I was forcing a screaming child to participate in a supposedly fun family ski race. After I got him to the starting line, he started loudly telling me that he wanted to "Kill the clowns. I don't want any more clowns, Mommy. I hate clowns!" We took off and at one point in the race, several clowns came near us and my son noticed them. He started screaming and jabbing his little pint-sized poles at the clowns, yelling, "I kill you. I don't like you!" I had to quickly grab him before he could hurt the clowns and tried to explain that he was just scared of clowns and costumed figures and then hurried to the finish while he alternately hid his head in my chest while shaking with fear and peeked out to tell the clowns that he wanted to kill them. I now have a large finish line poster of me carrying my son while he has a death grip on me and peeks out over my shoulder to take aim at the clowns to commemorate this family moment.

There have been so many other awkward mom moments that I have gotten used to it and no longer feel embarrassed, horrified or otherwise ashamed. I also know that more are to come, such as a recent son's drunken and high text from a party about how much fun he was having because he was so drunk and high. I now experience these moments as being humorous or ironic because, no matter what depth of knowledge and experience I develop, I realize that I will never know enough to accurately anticipate and prepare for every problem. I know that my children are going to be human beings who will continually surprise me. They have shown me all the little areas of false pride that I didn't realize were mine. They have taught me that pride is worthless for parents who want peace of mind. It is much better to let your kids strip you of your pride so you can stop pretending that you and they are all that. No one wants to feel pressure to be something they can never become. If you have an ounce of compassion for your own and your children's humanity, then you should let go of things going a certain cherished way, including your child not having a mental health diagnosis.

PARENT RESILIENCY RULE 2
Let go of things going the way you imagined with your child and let go of your dream that they never be anxious. Do this to make room for the person your child will become.

When I look back, the thing I really needed to help me avoid self-imposed insanity during the pregnancy and child rearing process was something that no one was talking about. I needed permission to get it wrong, permission for my kid to get it wrong and permission to surrender to the messy hilarity of being a parent. I needed a vocal group of parents willing to announce that no parent can perfect their parenting or perfect their children. No child can fulfill the vision of his parent's imagination. I needed at least one parent who could bravely stand up and shout that "Sh** happens and it is no one's fault!" I needed someone willing to say that it wasn't all my fault when things came out badly and likewise that it wasn't a credit to my parenting when things went well. I needed a pep talk that told me that I was going on an adventure into uncharted territory that would be simultaneously fascinating, amazing, horrifying, wonderful and disappointing. I needed someone to be the anarchist of parent perfection and over accommodation.

PARENT RESILIENCY RULE 3
Take the pressure off yourself and your child by allowing your child to take a long time to grow up and become skilled at being a human being.

Your first step in the journey to raising a resilient child full of self-worth who also happens to have an anxiety disorder is to give yourself and your child permission to fail and make mistakes. It is best if you pick the most embarrassing and most frustrating areas to target, since these are going to be the ones that bring out the most unhelpful thoughts and beliefs that undermine your and your child's ability to become truly resilient and joyful. Write down the three most likely to make you lose your cool situations that can happen with your child and reframe them as opportunities for growth for both yourself and your child. Reframe them as normal attempts to grow up human. Restate them as useful attempts to learn mastery of self and situation that all children deserve. Be compassionate about the inability of others to deeply understand your situation because they have not had to experience it for themselves. This is your opportunity to put the rules for resilient parents into practice. For example:

Situation	Reframe what this means for your child's growth	Reframe what it means for you
My daughter will never text or call her friends on her own. They have to reach out to her first.	Her social anxiety makes this difficult. I know that she wants to be able to feel comfortable with initiating social contact. I can help her best by having a plan for exposure practice and not harping on it every moment.	If I stay calm and matter of fact, I can show her that this is just a problem that can be solved with practice. If I have to get medication or more therapy to help her, then I will do it. She is also learning how to cultivate solitude and not getting caught up in fear of missing out by texting constantly.

Now, it's your turn. Be sure to pick the three situations that you find most embarrassing or frustrating.

Now that you have identified some of your unhelpful expectations and reframed them, you need to address the part of you that is likely to view yourself or your child as being a victim. This is very important. The extent to which you view yourself or your child as a victim of their problems is the degree to which you will disable yourself and your child in developing self-worth and great coping skills. Next, I will go over what happens when you get caught up in misperceiving yourself, your child or your family as being victims of anxiety or other things you never hoped for.

— CHAPTER 2 —

This Isn't What
I Signed Up For

The tendency to believe that you are clever and in control starts with pregnancy. You read everything you can find that tells you what will happen to your body, to the baby growing inside you. This gives you false confidence that makes you think, "I've got this. Haven't billions of parents already done this? If I just do the right things and avoid all of the wrong things, then everything will go really well." You might fantasize about the lovely birthing suites at your local hospital or about your meaningful home birth. Or you might fantasize about holding your newly born child, or the things that you will do together as a family. You get hypnotized by the lovely photos of pregnant and nursing moms, content dads beaming at their child peeking out from the frontpack, and the other beautiful images of parents playing with their children. You get fascinated by pregnancy blogs, journals, ways to help your partner during birth and birthing stories. You get caught up in the romance of becoming a parent. I did too.

I waited until after I finished six years of doctoral studies and passed my licensing exam before I even tried to get pregnant. I also had a history of being a very healthy athletic woman who was a competitive distance runner likely to pass the most rigorous physical that NASA has for its astronauts. When I read the pregnancy books, I read them like they were the guidebook of pregnancy that would allow me to exert maximal control over my pregnancy and postpartum experience.

The first clue during my first pregnancy that I had better revise my expectations was severe unremitting nausea, vomiting, heartburn and a bloodhound's ability to detect all odors. When my patients walked into my office, I could smell their deodorant, their shampoo, the food they had eaten and the perfume they wore. It was nauseating. I had many anxious moments of trying to suppress the urge to vomit when patients came near me. I had to suck on peppermints to try and fool my olfactory senses into believing that what I smelled was not overwhelming. I became a veritable fountain of vomit. All food smelled atrocious. I periodically had to run to the bathroom to vomit at work. I did the same at home and prayed that the second trimester would bring relief just like my doctor promised. This did not happen. I ended up vomiting right up until I pushed out my son. I was so nauseated and vomitous throughout my pregnancy that I lost weight, which made me worry about what was happening to the baby developing inside me.

Then, to add misery to pain, I had bleeding during the tenth week of pregnancy. Ultrasounds showed that my placenta was partially detached. I was put on bedrest for a month and told to move as little as possible. This was a form of torture for me because I am a very active person who has always loved being athletic and outdoorsy. I felt nauseous, scared for my baby and outrageously restless because the only "activity" I was allowed was five trips to the bathroom and some not too vigorous leg wiggling. My doctor kindly explained that my pregnancy might not be viable. I was able to continue working over the telephone which helped me maintain my sanity. At least my work life felt predictable when everything about being pregnant and having a uterus felt wildly out of control. I had never even heard of a placenta partially detaching and I worried about the possible effects of decreased blood flow to my baby's brain. All that graduate training in brain development and brain injury was like crack cocaine for my worry.

Eventually I was able to go back to work and I stopped worrying about placental tears and stunted brain development. Unfortunately, I started getting severe heartburn and asthma due to all the frequent vomiting. I had been vomiting so much that I had been inhaling some of the vomit into my lungs. (My apologies to those readers who just got grossed out.) I began constant violent coughing that often resulted in vomiting that no amount of medication could overcome. I could not stop coughing even when trying to sleep and both my husband and I became sleep deprived and cranky without having the benefit of a newborn to blame it on. I had an episode of such violent coughing that I broke a rib. That meant that any subsequent coughing and vomiting were excruciatingly painful. I also started getting pneumonia. (Note to reader. There is a happy ending to this story. You just might need an emotional seatbelt to finish this part of the ride. I certainly did.) My dream of being natural and not allowing any potentially harmful food or substance into my body went down the drain. I was having such a difficult time gaining weight that I ate the only things that nausea would allow, grape soda, grilled turkey Reuben sandwiches and fistfuls of colored tropical fruit antacid tablets.

Then, I had another partial tear of the placenta at 30 weeks and again at 32 weeks that had me staying in the hospital and at home on permanent bedrest until my baby made his way out of my body. I broke another rib from extreme vomiting and coughing. This happened the night I was supposed to start my labor and delivery classes. I was wheeled from the Emergency Department past the hospital classroom area that was to host my fellow classmates. I had been yearning to take these classes because they were part of my vision of being pregnant.

The realization that I was not going to attend my labor and delivery classes and would have to bypass the tour of the nursery and birthing suites felt like I was being robbed of all the good stuff. It also felt like the last straw. Possibly, like those of you who have had the misfortune of sharing my experience of high risk pregnancy, I felt like my body had betrayed me and fate had turned an experience that I had longed for into a constantly evolving nightmare. I remember sobbing in the maternity ward and telling my husband and the nurse something like "but how will we be able to have a good birth if we cannot go to the classes?! We don't even have a birth plan!" The nurse was very patient and explained that I was in the maternity ward and getting a much better look than if I had only gone on a half hour tour. She told me that I was getting to work with the same nurses who would help me deliver my baby so I should feel much more comfortable with the staff and facility than if I had only taken the classes. She also told me that what really mattered was having a good nurse and a doctor who was good at catching things like footballs and babies. She told me that my baby would be born whether or not I had a birth plan. She did something very important that I did not appreciate at the time. She showed me that every disadvantage has its advantages. There was no such thing as a perfect way to be pregnant or give birth. What really mattered was whether or not I had good resources when mine were absent. She was so right.

When labor finally arrived, I went to the hospital with no plan, no preconceptions and lots of confidence in the nurses. I just did what the nurses suggested and realized that the nurse was right. My son was going to be born and this required no skill on my part. I just had to be willing to go along. It felt terrific to finally get to the prize part of being pregnant, holding and nursing my baby for the first time. I know that I was fortunate compared to most moms because my perspective was already adjusting to the reality that motherhood was going to be a sort of rollercoaster ride through danger, fear, pain, joy and absurdity. I did not care that my son's APGAR (Appearance, Pulse, Grimace, Activity, and Respiration: the measurement of the newborn's status) scores were low. It did not matter that I had violated every preconceived notion of how I was going to have a healthy pregnancy. I was just glad that my son was alive and that I was no longer vomiting, coughing or in pain. I was in love with my son and was so achingly grateful that we were alive together. That was a precious moment of sweet wisdom and grace.

If you are willing to join me in sorting through your expectations for your children, yourself and your family, you have the opportunity to let go of ideals, myths and dreams that guarantee disappointment. Hanging on to your cherished ideal of what your experience, your child or your family should be sets you up for unnecessary grief. You cannot possibly correctly guess what is to come for yourself, your child or your family. Your intuition cannot possibly read all the nuances of your child's soul and predict who they will become. It is just not possible. Trying to keep yourself or your family on track with your ideal of how they should look, act and feel places you in a trap of self-doubt and despair. It sets you up to continually notice deviations from the ideal and falsely imagine the terrible things will happen when the ideal does not occur.

The problem for many parents is that we get caught up in trying to attain what we hoped for and overlook the blessing of the mess. My experience has taught me that mess is more likely to occur than ordered progression toward the thing I imagined. Mess can be magic and filled with great hilarity, fun and opportunities for growth when you choose to let go of things going the "right" way, and this includes your child without their anxiety.

Research on happiness shows that when children learn to enjoy and be grateful for the small daily moments of play, mastery and relationship versus chasing after accomplishments, material possessions and things going their way, then they experience a much higher level of satisfaction and joy (Keltner & Marsh, 2015). Letting go of your cherished ideals about parenting and child rearing will free you to enjoy the process of raising your children without being tortured by self-doubt, mistakes or the disapproval of others. If you release your unhelpful expectations, then you show your child how to ignore the unhelpful expectations of others. You show your child that their version of humanity is perfectly imperfect.

When I began my parent's journey, I naively assumed that my ability to be a therapist would spare me some of the frustrations and embarrassments that other moms experienced. I did not realize how painful it is to be the parent whose child is rarely admired by other parents or who never wins any awards. I did not understand how patronizing it would feel to have people repeatedly tell me how lucky my child was to have been born to two parents who were clinical psychologists. I quickly learned to randomly expect one of "those calls" from the principal or headmaster and to just give up the idea that my children were going to somehow be exceptional in a way that would be impressive to others. "Those calls" tended to start in one of two ways. "Normally we put kids in detention or suspension, but in your son's case..." or "We are calling to let you know that your child did something (fill in the blank with something really unusual, such as the time my third grade son was so startled by the fire drill bell that he peed in his pants, or the time my anxiety ridden son refused to sit near any kids at lunch because he was so socially anxious and depressed)." The first several times this happened, my face burned with shame because I so wanted my child to be the kid I had hoped for. Even though my intellectual professional psychologist self knew these events were to be expected, it still felt embarrassing. Secretly, I wanted to be the parent that other parents admired. I wanted my kids to be the one who every other parent wanted to invite to their house for playdates. That may happen to some parents, but it certainly did not happen to me.

The turnaround for me came when I started to enjoy the absurdity of my situation and realized that the best version of my children was the way they were, which I will describe in a later chapter. I dared to ask myself a profound and important question, "Why not me and why not my children?" I began to realize that I was living the life that all parents live. I needed to get on with loving the child I had rather than striving for a different version of my child. It was my good fortune and my children's good fortune that I got to figure out more quickly that no child should ever live under the pressure of their parent's fantasy vision, even when that fantasy vision is an anxiety-free life. The only really absurd thing about my life was my foolish belief that anything really impressive and photoworthy needed to happen in order for it to be good.

> **HOT TIP**
>
> Learn to ask yourself, "Why not me and my children?"

When I realized that my kids were going to be their own creations and not the image of my parental imagination, I decided that I might as well change my expectations. I started using a new phrase in my mind. "This is the new normal. Love what you have instead of pining after what you cannot have." Once I began doing this it allowed me to grieve the loss of my dream. I began to feel much less self-doubt and a great deal more good humor. I see this same pattern in the parents I see in my office. They feel more confident, more fulfilled and more productive when they embrace their child's anxiety disorder as the new normal, normal for their family. It was painful when I saw how neither of my sons were going to go to school dances because they were too socially anxious to ask or let anyone know they wanted to attend, whereas their two step-siblings had no anxiety about school dances and easily attended them. I had to take the focus off of disappointment and put it on coping and enjoying every little bit of good that could be had in the moment. Raising a child who is anxious most definitely has its fun, funny and joyful moments. Looking at the photo poster when my youngest meant to kill the clowns is now a source of laughter for my family.

The parents who are robust joyful paragons of parenting will tell you that parenting is a crazy quilt of experiences both joyful and sad, surprises both wonderful and wrenching and disappointments both great and small, no matter who you raise. The difference for you and me is that we get to figure this out sooner than the other parents who can maintain the illusion longer. You learn early to better appreciate the good and funny moments because you know they are precious. The sooner you adjust to this reality the sooner you can learn to cultivate joy, good humor and the ability to live well no matter what is going on with your child's anxiety.

PARENT RESILIENCY RULE 4
Love the child you have and not the one you hoped for.

Our current culture of parenting pushes us toward some profoundly unhelpful expectations (Pew Research Center, 2015). Women who were mothers forty to fifty years ago show that what good mothers used to expect of themselves were the following (Hardy, 2012):

- Keep the house tidy and clean.

- Feed the kids and partner.

- Raise kids who grow up to be people of good character who are honest, hardworking, pay their taxes and get jobs that allow them to move out from mom and dad's.

- Discipline and express your disapproval when they violate the rules of good conduct and good character.

Fathers of forty to fifty years ago were expected to earn enough money to provide adequate shelter, food, clothing and vacations (Hardy, 2012). They were also expected to teach their sons how to play sports, use tools and hand out discipline for severe infractions. Pretty simple.

Do you notice how simple that list looks and feels? When my mother was raising me, she had no expectation other than to police me and my sisters for signs of bad character when we lied, stole coins from her purse or hit each other on purpose. It never occurred to her that her children were supposed to like her, confide everything in her or that we had to like the meals she cooked. She felt empowered to send us out of the house as soon as we finished chores or homework because she did not want to do the extra cleaning or tidying up that having us being cooped up indoors entailed. She also knew that we loved playing outdoors and she did not worry about what we were up to when we were out of sight. She assumed that we would grow up with all of our limbs and faculties intact and that we did not need any enrichment activities to stimulate our brains and that we would be safe enough without her and needed to play with other kids in order to be happy and healthy. She also assumed that we would learn to work our way through conflicts with other kids and teachers. It did not occur to her that she should help us do homework, only that she should make sure we got it done. If we couldn't do it, she just told us to go back and ask the teacher. She also felt fine appearing in public without makeup or nice clothes because dressing up was something you only did for church, fancy nights out or military balls.

My father worked hard, made and saved money and enforced discipline or gave us "the talking to" when we misbehaved. He was unusual because he attended all of our school or sporting events, which were usually just attended by the moms because the dads were either working or relaxing after a day of work. He was the one who did play wrestling with us, taught us sports and taught us how to mow the lawn when we were large enough to push the lawn mower. He was also the one who would be sure to explain what good character meant and how we were failing to exhibit good character when we misbehaved or treated others poorly.

I cannot recall my mom playing with me and neither can my sisters. I do not recall any of my friend's mothers playing with any of us. I also do not recall my mom trying to help me make friends even though my father was in the military and we moved every six to eighteen months. Looking back, I now know that I suffered from diagnosable generalized anxiety and social anxiety disorder but no one acted as though something was wrong with me or suggested that my shyness or ability to worry and have trouble sleeping limited my future. I enjoyed my childhood because I was left to my own devices and was free of the pressure to be happy, successful, admirable or well developed. Although I now have a PhD, it never occurred to me that I could make straight As until I accidentally made mostly As in seventh grade and realized that it was within my capability. I am sure that somewhere in some ancient infant school files, there are descriptors of me that showed absolutely no academic promise nor giftedness. None. No one told me to study hard or told me that I should be doing better in school. I discovered being a good student on my own and it became my own thing that represented me as I wanted to be.

Contrast this with what happens to many parents today. Pre-pregnancy blogs and books tell you all the things you should do so you give birth to a bright and healthy baby by doing everything the right way. Pregnancy books and blogs alarm you with all the things you need to avoid in order to prevent something terrible happening. The number of rituals that you have to observe in order to properly experience and document your pregnancy has become vast. You are even expected to have a gender reveal party with a surprising and clever way of indicating the gender of your child. While I agree that every mother should avoid substance abuse, smoking and alcohol during pregnancy, I do not agree with getting wound up about every morsel of food, body product and aerosol because this turns pregnancy and parenting into an endless list of alarming rules and needless efforts to get it just right. No one can have a perfect pregnancy or be a perfect parent. This emphasis on detecting and preventing all danger to your baby is unfair to your mental health and that of your child. It is especially unfair to those of you who have anxious kids because the assumption up front is that you did not adequately protect your child from disability or poor mental health. One of the most frequent fears I hear from parents is wondering if they could have done something different during pregnancy or early childhood to prevent their child's anxiety disorder. They assume they could have prevented a problem if only they had done everything perfectly. This is not only incorrect, it also sets you on a needless path of self-blame about something over which you had no control.

The emphasis on preventing harm has become so pervasive that parents are afraid to allow their children to play alone in the yard, to walk alone in the neighborhood or simply to walk to the nearest playground. It also means that parents avoid letting their kids play with other kids who appear to be challenging. It puts us at a disadvantage when we are trying to create opportunities for growth and friendship because our children who are anxious are misperceived as being quieter, more active, more irritable or more whiney than other kids and therefore less desirable. It pressures us to feel more false shame because we cannot always make our children pass for ideal.

The cultural message is now loud and clear that parents who fail to prevent the unlikeliest of harm or perceived misbehavior are criminal or derelict. Instead of our culture supporting parents and helping them deal with the random tragedies and accidents that no parent can ever predict or prevent, we criminalize and vilify the mother whose child breaks their arm, gets in an automobile accident, has a drug overdose or accidentally gets caught in the machinery of the escalator and dies (Rodriguez, 2019). Instead of compassion and an acknowledgment that random tragedy can happen to anyone, society condemns the parent who suffers random harm to their child. This harmful expectation creates an enormous and terrible responsibility that no parent should bear. It creates the myth that the really good parents are the ones whose kids come to no harm and who do not deviate from the comfortable path of predictability. It also leads to the belief that good mothers do not have children who have struggles with their mental health, such as anxiety disorders. Just as I could not secure the perfect pregnancy for my firstborn, I cannot secure a future for my child that protects him from all crime, all tragedy, mean people, unfair teachers and people who are lazy, or even *from his own anxiety*. My only good choice is to prepare my children for the rough and tumble of life and acknowledge that although I can influence my children's development, I can never control or guarantee a good outcome. Never. This attitude, in turn, helps my child accept their anxiety disorder and the inevitable challenges of life.

What else is expected of parents in our current culture

of parenting out of fear? Surveys of parents during the past decade show that the expectations have changed. Mothers who are good now are often supposed to do the following:

- Always make really healthy meals and provide healthy snacks.

- Always do whatever seems to create secure emotional attachment, such as breastfeed for several years, wear your baby in a sling or wrap, co-sleep and spend lots of time reassuring your child of your love.

- Always create artistic and Instagram-worthy parties, home interiors and holiday themed decorations.

- Always do things that enrich your child's brain development by reading to them every night, signing your child up for enrichment classes starting in infancy, enrolling them in the best preschools and schools that ideally leads to admission to prestigious upper schools and universities.

- Always make sure your parenting is green by avoiding disposable diapers, plastics and junky food, attempting to grow your own food and clothe your child in natural fabrics and use toys made of sustainable materials.

- Raise children who excel at various interests, hobbies and academics.

- Always have such a close trusting relationship with your child(ren) such that they confide in you at all times, never lie and seek your advice.

- Always prevent all possible injuries, disabilities or accidental harm or death of any of your children.

- Regarding mums – always maintain a thin, sexy appearance that looks as though you never gave birth to children and always be interested in sex because your relationship with your partner is hot and wonderful.

- Always be able to boast about something marvelous and exceptional that your child has done in comparison to other children.

Fathers who are good are often expected to do the following:

- Always look athletic instead of having a "Dad bod."

- Attain a large income that can finance home ownership, enrichment sports, arts and activities for the kids, catered parties, high end "safe" baby products and furniture, access to the "best" schools, college tuition, retirement savings and vacations at theme parks and resorts, and provide quality clothing, toys and healthy foods, preferably organic.

- Always assist with house chores and all aspects of child rearing.

- Always spend quality time with the children each day.

- Always participate in pregnancy and lactation classes and be helpful during the birthing process.

- Always have useful hobbies that might include crafting home brewed beers, liquors or wines, organic gardening, be competent at sports, afford fine cigars.

- Always advance through a career that provides ever increasing income to accommodate increased spending on homes, possessions, entertainment and vacations.

I bet if you re-read this list you will recognize the origins of your unhelpful inner parent fantasies and self-recriminations about being a parent. If the list looks overwhelming to you, it is. If you try to adhere to many of these ideals, then you are doomed to need therapy for anxiety and depression. So are your kids. The hard part for you is daring to become the cultural rebel who declares themselves subject to a new set of rules because you realize these expectations are absurd and do not fit you or your children. I speak with many parents who want to let go of these expectations but fear that, if they do, they will put their kids at a disadvantage by not giving in to these cultural pressures. It takes courage and clarity of vision to be the one who says, "Enough of this insanity! I am only one small human and so is my child. We will figure it out as we go and have fun along the way. We do not have to worry about the imagined awful future. We are going to take pleasure in what we can enjoy now so we do not waste a moment!"

So, if you want to begin your journey of letting go of expectations that hurt you and your family, let's start by identifying all the things that set you up for unnecessary disappointment.

First, take a look at the list of things twenty-first-century parents think they should do and be. Take a close look at the ones that apply to you. Select your answers based upon what you secretly think you and your kids should be, even though you might also realize it does not fit. Simply stating the truth about which cultural pressures you may have accidentally succumbed to can help you see your vulnerable zones that you will need to protect from outside and inside pressure.

- Look thin/be at pre-baby weight.

- Look my best when outside the house.

- Look great in a swimsuit.

- Have others admire my body because I am in such good shape.

- Have no stretch marks, cellulite, double chins or love handles.

- Look good enough so that no editing is needed when I post photos.

- Always make really healthy meals.

- Always provide healthy snacks.

- Never feel resentment or hatred toward my children.

- Never doubt myself for having given birth to my child.

- Never yell at my child in anger.

- Never slap, hit or push my child in anger and never feel the urge to slap, hit or push.

- Never swear at my child or swear because of my child.

- Always stay calm whenever my child is losing their temper.

- Create quality family time each day or at least each week.

- Raise children who want to go to church, temple, mosque or other religious services.

- Enjoy helping my children with schoolwork, science projects or holiday projects.

- Maintain my interest in sex and have sex as frequently as I did when first married/partnered.

- Maintain my makeup/hair/beard routine like I did before having children.

- Have special heart to heart talks and cuddles with my kids after they misbehave.

- Be able to afford anything that my children need and much of what they want.

- Have enough money to live in the best public school district or to be able to afford a private school.

- Have special family vacations that everyone enjoys and remembers with great fondness.

- Be able to take my children to fancy theme parks, such as Walt Disney World.

- Be a stay at home parent without jeopardizing our financial circumstances.

- Have kids who reach developmental milestones earlier than other kids.

- Have kids who learn numbers, letters, reading and math faster than other kids.

- Have kids who are put in advanced or accelerated classes.

- Have kids who the teachers really do like better than other kids.

- Have kids who get invited to all the birthday parties, sleepovers and kid gatherings.

- Have kids who attend all the birthday parties, sleep-overs and kid gatherings.

- Have kids who get excited about my birthday, parents' day or the holidays and remember to get or make me gifts and do special things for me.

- Have kids who never lie to me.

- Have kids who grandparents admire.

- Have kids that get asked on dates or to school dances.

- Have kids who excel in at least one area outside of school.

- Have kids who love to read.

- Have kids who always get their homework done.

- Have kids who never get into trouble with school staff, neighbors, grandparents or other parents.

- Have kids who never get into trouble with drugs or alcohol.

- Have kids who get into top notch colleges that others admire.

- Have kids who are happy and have good self-esteem.

- Have kids who do not have any mental health prob-lems or diagnoses.

- Have kids who do not need special education services, therapists or doctors other than for allergies.

- Have kids who win some awards for achievement or excellence.

Now, I want you to begin the process of undermining and discarding this list of mental chains. List your favorite fantasy images of how you hoped you would be with your children, what would happen and how you and others should react. Take the time to recall your daydreams about your children, what you long for and what you fear might not happen. Then underneath each one, write a reframe that is realistic that allows for mistakes, anxiety, disappointment and your and your child's humanity. This reframe should focus upon normalizing the inevitable and what might be the opportunity in the situation. If you get it right, you will feel your worry decrease and your heart expand into the emotional relaxation room you just created inside yourself. Here are some of the cherished secret fantasies that I had before I realized they were unhelpful.

Example: I imagine what it will be like to get called by the principal to come to the awards ceremony so I can watch my child get a special award.

Reframe: Of course, it would be nice to have my kid get awards, but since when does that guarantee success in life? What if my kids are good people but just don't happen to be the ones who get awards? Does that really mean that they and I have failed?

Example: I picture myself participating in a mommy–son book club and all the boys become really interested in reading.

Reframe: Sure, this sounds nice, but what if your son does not think this is fun? Isn't it more important to cultivate some shared interests and hobbies you can both enjoy? You might need to learn how to play video games or how to enjoy riding bikes together.

Example: I picture my child having lots of good friends and being the one who never gets picked on.

Reframe: Whoa there! Kids learn how to be good friends by making mistakes and 70 percent of seventh graders engage in bullying behavior. Chances are that my child will have both good friendships and the not so great friendships they outgrow. What kind of resilient human being would they be if all their relationships were easy? They would never learn how to handle conflict, rejection and frustration. They are going to need to learn by experience.

Example: I picture my child being kind to other children and never sexting or doing mean things to other kids.

Reframe: If I raise my child right by teaching them to handle peer pressure and to be self-disciplined and make good decisions that work toward their future, I can lower the likelihood of these things happening but I can never get rid of the possibility. I need to accept that most kids make mistakes in these areas and why not my kids? I need to be prepared to help them navigate these hurdles when they occur without driving them away from me with shame, disapproval and shock. I need to start talking to them now about handling the urge to be mean and impulsive and how to not take the mean remarks of others so seriously.

— CHAPTER 3 —

Grab the Fun Whenever You Can

Raising an anxious child can be challenging. If you are like the parents I work with, and like me, then you might have to deal with some routine joy killers. It can be frustrating to have to attend therapy, to get your child to take medication and to deal with the reaction of others who do not understand why your child is having a major meltdown yet again. It can get repetitive to explain why your child does not want to go on the class field trip because they are scared of thunderstorms or of getting lost. When you have a child with an anxiety disorder you have extra activities and extra things to keep track of that other parents get to skip. In your zeal to be a great parent who rises to the occasion, you might make the mistake that I and so many others have made by becoming "Theraparents," the parents whose lives revolve around being heroic and getting the job done right. Let me illustrate by what happened to me the first several years of my firstborn's life. I have observed the same process in the majority of parents I work with who accidentally become masters of accommodation by trying to make sure that everything is just right for their child.

When my firstborn arrived, I knew that he was an answer

to prayer after a difficult pregnancy. I delighted in his perfectly gorgeous thick shock of wavy auburn hair that made him look like a baby with a toupee. I imagined him growing up becoming a red-haired professor, pastor, leader or scientist. When I learned that he had cerebral palsy, I still imagined that he would be a clumsy but academically gifted boy. Why? Because the genetic relatives I knew of from my family were all very good at school even when they had other mental health or social problems. I overlooked the fact that my husband's family had a much more varied background with respect to academic achievement and finishing diplomas. I overlooked the fact that no mother has control over the version of human they birth into the world.

The first sign that my expectations were misguided happened when my firstborn son was unable to learn the alphabet in preschool and kindergarten. He loved school and was a happy little dude. He just couldn't do the same academic things that other kids did. Doctor appointments, testing and evaluations revealed that he had severe ADHD and an array of severe learning disabilities that meant he was functioning like a mildly cognitively impaired kid even though he had above average vocabulary and great social intelligence. It meant that we had to start him on ADHD medications at age three because he had such difficulty staying focused on any one task. He would begin trying to pull on his coat and then, with his coat halfway over his head, crawl over to play with a toy if he happened to be distracted by that same toy while in the middle of putting on his coat. Many years later, he is still like this even though he has had years of attention training and medication. It is just the way his brain functions.

The behavioral psychologist in me saw these initial disabilities as a challenge, like climbing the Mount Everest of motherhood. The perfectionist in me wanted to believe that my son could become one of those terrific overcoming disabilities stories. I remembered that when my firstborn was still an infant, I watched a TV show about a young man born with no arms who became a college conference wrestling champion. I vowed to be the type of mother I imagined this young man had. I imagined that she was a mom who saw the diamond in the rough and encouraged her son to develop all of his potential despite his missing limbs. I even made a video to my son shortly after learning he was disabled. I tearfully told him that I would do everything I could to help him become his better self as I imagined it and would fight to get him into the college of his choice, disabilities be damned! I also was careful to avoid the use of the word "disabled" in case my son felt stigmatized. I was careful to use the politically correct term "differently abled" or to just talk as though every kid had to go to physical therapy, speech therapy and occupational therapy four days a week. Had you asked me, I would have said that my son was perfectly normal, thank you, and he also happened to have a few rough spots in his development. I mentally avoided thinking about the possibility that he would not do all the same things that other kids do and that he might forever appear to be different and be in real need of supportive care. I had the naive belief that with enough effort, any child of mine would overcome disability if they had the best intervention and a mother willing to do her part. If you are like most of my patients with anxious children, then you might recognize yourself in these beliefs.

My worst problem was that I knew too much and it scared me. I knew that failure to do the proper intervention early in a child's life could result in lost opportunities for achieving a more independent lifestyle. My professional training told me that the earlier and more thoroughly I intervened, then the more likely my son would achieve certain critical developmental milestones. I knew that failure to achieve certain milestones meant that my son would never develop normally. Since his pediatrician had delayed telling us that she suspected cerebral palsy until he was eighteen months old, I felt that we had to rush to make up for lack of therapy during the first eighteen months of my son's life. I felt like I was in a race to save his future normal self.

I attacked this challenge like I was training for the Olympics of parenthood. Each therapist gave me stacks of handouts with recommended home exercises, special ways to adapt the house to meet my son's needs and a long list of bad habits to avoid because it might result in failure to use his muscles properly. I even had to stop guessing what my son meant and force him to attempt to use speech instead of flailing, grunting and pointing. I was told that he would never develop normal speech unless I made him make the effort to acquire speech. He hated that. I remember trying to be patient for a long ten minutes of tantrum when he pointed at a toy on top of the shelf that he wanted me to give him. I kept insisting he use speech. He kept yelling and pointing toward the toy. After a back and forth battle of "Tell me with words" and yells and grunts and pointing, he finally gave in and yelled for the first time, in a very angry and distinct voice, "Mis Stir Poe Tay Toe Head!" Had he been familiar with the F-bomb, I am confident that he would have said that too.

I have always loved being organized, so I created a giant three-inch-wide binder containing all of the handouts from therapists, my notes and other articles on my son's problems. This binder became the Bible of our lives. Every waking moment was dedicated to being therapeutic. Here is an example of dinner time. "Sit this way, not that way. Hold onto the spoon instead of eating with your hands. Take smaller bites so you learn to keep the food in your mouth instead of cramming too much in your mouth. Drink this milk with thickener so you don't inhale thinner liquids that give you repeated respiratory infections. Tuck your chin when you swallow so you don't accidentally inhale your food or milk. If you want more, you have to say, 'more.'" My son then grunts and points at the extra food. Then I say, "Say more." My son then waves his hand toward the food. I say, "What do you need to say?" My son then gives me an annoyed look and says, "MMMM rrr." I put more food on his special adapted bowl and try to have polite dinner conversation, only he attempts to grab a fistful of food without trying to use his special spoon because it is so hard to hold the spoon without spilling the food. Then we repeat the entire process again. And again.

This was just mealtime. I adapted the entire house and all the toys to fit his special needs. If there was something a therapist suggested, then I made it happen. Our house became a homeschooling Harvard University version of physical therapy, speech therapy and occupational therapy. I also began researching medical libraries for information and new interventions. I ordered and studied graduate textbooks in occupational therapy and developmental delays. I remember thinking that I would do anything possible to help my son overcome his disabilities. All of this effort earned me praise from my son's therapists who would tell me things like "You are such a great mother! I have never seen someone do such a great job with the home program. Your son is so lucky to have you." Their compliments made me feel like I was really on track for helping my son outgrow his disabilities.

During this time, I also worked fulltime running my own

anxiety disorders practice, seeing patients, supervising my staff and students and giving presentations. I loved my professional work. It also gave me a respite from my home life in which I felt constantly worried about my son's development. During the two years after my son's diagnosis, I felt like I was racing to beat the developmental clock so my son could become the vision of a normal academically gifted klutzy sort of boy that I had seen in the posters of kids of The Cerebral Palsy Foundation. I overlooked the science that showed that the majority of kids with brain injuries like my son's are often significantly cognitively impaired and suffer many mental health and academic problems. I kept hoping that my son would be one of the ones whose muscles were just a bit off. I assumed he would be a great student, a college standout and a kid who would amaze us all. The reality, however, was the exact opposite of my fantasy. Each year seemed to bring another diagnosis, another developmental delay and more information that suggested that my son's brain injury had affected much more than his muscles.

Then, like many of the parents I work with, I also became uncharacteristically sick with every cold, flu and virus. I repeatedly developed pneumonia, uncharacteristically gained forty pounds and looked like I had aged twenty years. Several people even came up to me asking if I was expecting another child because of my weight gain. I started getting acne for the first time in my life during these first two years of being a "Theraparent." So, when my husband got the opportunity to speak at a conference at Walt Disney World, I jumped at the chance to join him with our son. It did not even occur to me that I needed a vacation. I was focused upon having my son experience the magic of Disney.

My only dilemma was what about therapy? What would

happen if my son went an entire week without physical therapy, occupational therapy or speech therapy? What if he got behind! That meant I had better take the big binder along, right? But when it came time to fit everything into our bags, the binder did not fit. So, I carried the binder under the same arm that was also gripping the stroller and holding onto the diaper bag draped over my shoulder. I was not going to leave that binder behind. It felt like my insurance for preventing developmental disaster while on vacation.

If you have ever traveled to Walt Disney World with a young child, then you know the excruciating tension of handling a child's wild excitement about meeting Mickey while your child is simultaneously being disappointed by how long the trip to see Mickey is taking. It took several plane rides and several bus trips to get to our hotel on the Disney property. It took long enough that I began to worry about failing to do a single therapeutic thing with my son during the day. I had just let him sit any way he wanted and shove food into his mouth without taking precautions to avoid choking or inhaling food. I just tried to survive the experience of being asked every other minute when we would see Mickey Mouse and the embarrassment of knowing that the person sitting in front of us was repeatedly being bumped by my son's climbing in and out of his seat every five seconds.

When we arrived at our hotel room, we discovered that it had sliding glass doors that faced onto the kiddie pool which my son immediately spotted. I began unpacking and wondering which exercises from his binder I should do to make up for lost time. My son had other ideas. He raced to the sliding glass door and pushed aside the sheer curtain and began patting the glass and calling, "Mama! Mama! Mama!" I looked out at the pool and had the same thought he did.

"That looks like fun!" I dropped the binder and put on both our bathing suits and took him out to the pool.

We sat in the shallow water and warm sun and my son began laughing and splashing and thrashing with the sheer joy of being in such an amazing place. His laughter and splashing were so contagious that I began laughing and splashing too because it made him so happy. We sat there in the shallow water with my son propped between my legs laughing and splashing and having the best time of our lives.

And then it hit me, this was the first time since my son's diagnosis that we were just having fun. I was just loving my son as he was without worrying about how to improve his motor skills or how to somehow reduce his disability. I was just sitting in the warm sun and water and enjoying the moment. Once I realized this I began to cry.

Then I realized that I hated that binder. I realized that my son hated that binder. He just was too good natured to tell me. I realized that I hated the way I had been living. I realized that I hated all the relentless expectations to improve my son and to improve my parenting and to create a life that was somehow better than the one I was living. I realized that I had just spent the past two years being caught up in a relentless pursuit of perfect parenthood and perfect rehabilitation of disability. I was in the middle of Walt Disney World and I had been planning on turning the Magic Kingdom into the Therapy Kingdom!

I had gotten stuck in the same hamster wheel of perfectionism that destroys parenthood for so many parents. I had the hubris to believe that if I did my job right, then my son would turn out right. I lost sight of all the most important lessons that my son needed to learn. He needed to learn that I loved him just the way he was, in the moment as it was, without having to somehow improve it, or manage it to make it better. I then vowed to begin loving him the way he was and to learn to love the moment the way it was without trying to improve it, manage it or make it lead to my imagined better future.

I lost sight of my own humanity and, in doing so, lost sight of my son's humanity. My well-intentioned micromanagement, which I justified by pointing to my son's disabilities and the therapists' instructions, was no more than the same unhelpful micromanagement and overparenting that many other parents do. They just use a different justification. "So my child will do better in school. So my child will have better self-esteem when they are around other kids. So my child will not feel left out. So my child will see how special they are. So my child will have the same chances as other kids." I was just pretending to myself and others that it was OK for me to overparent and overprotect because my child was disabled and therefore an exception to the research that shows how damaging overparenting is to a child's long-term mental health and success in life (Liu *et al.*, 2019).

This realization that I had just spent the past two years being and achieving the very opposite of what I ought to be doing as a parent shocked me into action. I threw out the binder and left it in the garbage bin at Walt Disney World. I decided that the best therapy to be had in Walt Disney World was to delight in the magic of watching my son be a kid in the middle of kids' paradise. I just let him be. I quickly discovered that I loved just letting him be and so did my son. The daily tantrums over being pushed to improve abruptly stopped and mealtimes became fun times. Ironically, my life began feeling much more normal when I stopped caring about my son trying to become normal. When I chucked the binder into the dust bin, I also chucked out my dreams of how things should be and oriented my compass toward whatever the present moment offered, disabilities be damned.

For the first time in two years, I let go of worrying about what the therapists wanted and dropped the pressure to be a perfect parent and the pressure to help my son improve. I let go of all the expectations that looked good on paper and filled a three-inch-wide binder. I decided that the most important thing that needed to happen was to express my delight in my son's presence, my son's zany not quite typical way of being in the world and in our zany definitely not normal life. I decided to accept that he was disabled and socially anxious and that there was nothing I could do to change that. I needed to show him that there was joy, fun and great mirth in the middle of disability, anxiety, imperfection and struggle. I needed to show him that the only real disability is the endless pursuit of the best and the most normal.

I discovered that when I focused upon my son's fun and delighted reaction to Walt Disney World without comparing it to the way other kids walked, talked and moved, it was a big bold blast of joy that made me weep with the privilege of being able to give this to my son. Hearing and seeing and feeling his delight, his way of moving with thrashing and disorganized movements, his inarticulate speech, his wide smiles and his profusion of drool was truly fun. He was my beautiful son having an experience of joy unadulterated by my pressure to improve and meet some milestone. Whether you realize it or not, your child is like mine. Your child comes in the package of a kid with anxiety and they are still beautiful.

HOT TIP

When things are fun, enjoy it for all it is worth! Enjoy every good and fun moment that occurs because you know they are precious gems in a life that also has anxiety and struggle.

This experience showed me that overfocus upon progress and therapy can kill joy even though it seems like such a good idea at the time. You need to be able to enjoy your child as you raise them, especially when they have the challenge of an anxiety disorder that will make them focus upon what is negative, scary and what might go wrong. Your child needs to see that you delight in their joy and in their presence without the pressure to perform all of the time. Your child is going to have repeated encounters with you and their therapy team that will be pushing them to do things that seem impossible. Necessary pushing to overcome fear will be part of your child's life. You and your entire family will need to learn that, even in the midst of life's difficulties, there is fun, laughter and great joy to be shared that does not require waiting until everything has been sorted out.

Research shows that people who notice what is positive and comment about it can improve the productivity of those around them by up to 31 percent (Achor, 2010). Studies on children who notice what went well and why it went well are much more likely to achieve in all areas of their life. Children who learn to be fully present in the moment and aware of what gives them pleasure and joy are more likely to have good mental health as adults. Also, children and adults recall best the things that are associated with laughter and good humor (Bains *et al.*, 2014; Posner *et al.*, 2014). Research shows that fun, joy and noticing the positive make it easier to learn to overcome any difficulty. One of the problems for children who suffer from anxiety disorders is that they spend less time doing truly fun things because their condition interferes with their ability to engage in spontaneous play or socializing. Anxiety makes them more serious, more negative in their focus and more risk avoidant. Children with anxiety disorders are also very likely to have parents who themselves have an anxiety disorder. If you add having a worried, depressed and overly serious parent into the mix of family culture, then life can get really grim. My experience with parents like you is that both you and your child could use a big dose of fun and joy in your life to cut the weight of worry. Our kids need to get their daily dose of joy and delight, and so do we, if we are to be mentally well in the midst of living and parenting a child with an anxiety disorder.

So, let's get to work on improving your ability to experience joy and delight with your child by doing the following exercises.

1. The next time you have to do something "therapeutic" with your child, take a moment to gaze into their eyes and just smile and enjoy each other. Spend some time admiring your child, savoring what is beautiful and unique about them and share your observation. "I just love the faded jeans blue of your eyes," or "You have the most fun laugh."

2. Plan a regular "nothing therapeutic/no rules/no stress" time to just be together and do something that *your*

child thinks is fun. Do this without interruption, without an agenda and without a plan. It can be eating everyone's favorite food together and watching a show, or sitting outside, or biking together. It can be watching them play dress up or a video game. The idea is to share something that is fun for your child while having a high tolerance for things that might go wrong. This teaches your child how to enjoy and seek fun for the sake of having fun.

3. Start keeping a journal of daily things that delight you about your child. This is especially helpful when your child is a preteen or a teen and they have lost their younger child cuteness and can say foul words or sulk in a ferocious manner. This will help train your brain away from focusing upon what is wrong. Our brains are hardwired to want to first notice negative and anxiety provoking information. We have to work to retrain them to pay attention to good things so we can have good mental health and teach our kids by our example.

4. Start asking your child what they are enjoying when they are in fun situations. Listen well and just enjoy the experience with them. Try to see the fun from their point of view and let them savor it with you. Use your questions to help draw their attention to what is good, fun and delightful each day.

5. Start smiling more and showing a friendly calm demeanor when your child shows their symptoms of anxiety. Take on the attitude, "Of course you are anxious. You have an anxiety disorder and that is

frustrating but is never a reason we cannot have a good day." Casually validate your child's anxiety and redirect them to notice what good might come of the situation. For example, "Looks like you are worrying a lot about school. I know you always end up passing your exams and I bet you can get better at managing your worry so school feels more fun," or "Looks like you're getting really scared about something bad happening to mom and dad when we go out. I know that the more you practice playing with your toys with the babysitter, then the sooner you will start learning how to have fun when we are gone."

6. Remind yourself that there is no other ideal version of your child, such as your child not having an anxiety disorder. Anxiety disorders are chronic and cannot be switched off. You can recover and become asymptomatic, but you never lose the tendency to become anxious when life stressors, illness or trauma happens. Children who manifest symptoms of anxiety disorders in childhood are very likely to experience repeated episodes of anxiety throughout their lives. Their best strategy for healthy living is to learn to detect symptoms early and take immediate action to engage in exposure practice and/or adjust their medications. The ideal version of a child's life with an anxiety disorder is to become a quick and efficient manager of symptoms in a matter of fact low key manner so you both have the energy to enjoy the blessings of your life with gusto. Gracefully accept that future anxiety episodes are going to be part of life and believe that each episode is an opportunity for important personal growth.

7. When you are tempted to feel sorry for your child, yourself or your family, learn to ask yourself "Why not me? Why not my child? Why not my family?" This will help to shift your perspective from feeling victimized into recognizing that your child is one of millions who had no choice in the genetics pool about being born into a life with an anxiety disorder. A victim is someone who receives unfair persecution. There is nothing unfair about whether or not a child develops an anxiety disorder just like there is nothing unfair about a child having blue eyes or black hair color. Anxiety disorders are a fact of the synergistic effect between genetics and environment. Anxiety disorders remind us that suffering and mental health conditions are a normal part of life for many. You are in good company, because anywhere from a third to almost one half of the human population in Australia, the United Kingdom and the United States of America experiences a mental health condition during their lifetime (Australian Government Department of Health, 2009; Marques de Miranda *et al.*, 2020; Steel *et al.*, 2014). Twenty-five percent of the population experienced an anxiety disorder prior to the COVID-19 pandemic and since the pandemic the rate has risen to 41 percent or more, especially for children and youth under the age of 25 (Kelley, 2020). Remembering these facts helps to reestablish healthy humility and acceptance.

PARENT RESILIENCY RULE 5

Give up being a "Theraparent" who overfocuses upon rapid and correct progress and embrace returning to being the parent who embraces the messy hilarity of your child's life.

— CHAPTER 4 —

Compassion and the New Normal

One of the most painful moments for me as a therapist is when I meet with a family for the first time and I see the parents getting teary-eyed or weeping when the assessment confirms the diagnosis of an anxiety disorder. It is also heart-breaking to see parents getting teary-eyed when their child or teen reveals a plethora of symptoms the parents did not realize were present. I know when I see those tears that these parents are feeling a mixture of grief for the lost anxiety-free future they assumed was their child's, guilt for not realizing how much their child suffered and fear that their child will never live the good life they imagined for their child's future.

Contrast this with what I see in their children. Typically, the more questions I ask and the more I tell children about their peers who have anxiety disorders, the more they reveal and the more relieved they look. They are often surprised that they are not the only one who has their symptoms and encouraged that I have worked with children like them who recovered from their symptoms. They may not like the idea of exposure therapy that entails facing the things they fear, but they are often interested in considering the idea if it means getting better. Most children I see, whether they are four years old or in their emerging adult years, take a practical approach once they discover that they are not unusual and that something constructive can be done to alleviate their daily struggle with anxiety.

The same is true for children who need to take medications. They are very practical in many instances. Even the preteen children who are most likely to balk at doing things adults prefer and who like to demonstrate their independence by disliking what adults like are intrigued with the idea of doing an experimental trial of therapy or medication to see if it can work for them. The thing that they do not like, however, is seeing their parent's distress. Frequently I see kids squirm when they see their parents' worry and tears. They know that the worry is about them. When I see them in private, they often tell me things like "I got really scared about my anxiety when I saw my mom cry," or "They never think I can do anything. I hate it when my dad gets all worried about whether or not I am going to get over my anxiety." I have even had one kindergartener tell me, "I thought it was just my silly mind telling me to not touch anything, but when I saw mom get so scared, I had to not let her see me not touching things!" In other words, this little girl misinterpreted her mother's worried reaction to her compulsions as a reason to hide her symptoms to avoid distressing her parent.

Your child has a practical concern and an emotional need. Your child wants to get better and they want to do it now. They also want to see the proof of your confidence that they can get better. They feel humiliated, ashamed or worried when they see you worry about them or about their progress. They are not able to grasp that your worry reflects your deep love. Instead, they misunderstand your worry as lack of confidence in their ability to overcome. They need you to show them how to recover while demonstrating your faith in their ability to get tough with anxiety. Think about this for a moment. When your parents remind you to drive safely and to call them when you get home to prove that you arrived safely, don't you feel the tiniest bit annoyed because you know that your driving record is good? Does their worry make you feel warm and fuzzy with all that expressed love? I know that when I went home after my first year of college and my father kept reminding me to check my phone messages and return calls I nearly started a family version of World War III because I felt so irritated and insulted. It didn't occur to me until thirty years later that he was just worrying about me getting a job and trying to be loving.

Casting off your attitude of worry and grief can become your secret weapon as a parent. One reason I and my staff can often get children and teens to do very difficult exposure tasks is because we are not giving off the signal that we are worried about their ability to improve. We know they will get better. We know that even the most severely impaired child or teen can make progress and overcome their anxiety. We also think it is fun to be the one who leads a child to successful mastery of anxiety. We communicate that joy and "no big deal about the challenge" feeling when we are working with a child. Quite frankly, it feels absolutely wonderful to do my job. It is a privilege to be the one who helps to transform a child's fear into mastery. So, when I enter my office and meet a family for the first time, I am feeling excited and happy about working with them. I would like to believe that the kids I work with sense this optimism and belief in their better selves and they respond to it, even when they are being dragged into my office. It is very difficult to feel discouraged when someone acts and talks like they truly believe that you have a better life ahead of you and that you can become great at getting there.

> ### PARENT RESILIENCY RULE 6
> Believe in your child's better self, the strong resilient self that can face and endure suffering only to become stronger and more capable.

I also know that the other secret ingredient that I have is compassion for their plight. I know that no human being wants to live with anxiety, that anxiety disorders can be crippling and very painful. I know that families come to my clinic because they have exhausted their resources. I can look each child, teen or parent in the eye and say both that "I see and feel your struggle and overwhelm *and* I believe you are the very one that can learn your way out of it. I am here by your side to help you get to your better self." Children and parents realize that they are well understood, both in their suffering and in their need to achieve personal greatness about living well with anxiety. This is what your child needs from you, not just their therapist. I am confident that if you give your child this perspective, you will need to spend fewer hours with mental health professionals like me.

If you have ever been the lucky recipient of an adult's compassionate mentoring, then you probably have fond memories of a favorite teacher, mentor, coach, supervisor or relative who was able to love you with clear-eyed compassion. You thrived because you knew that this special adult saw and understood all of you and that you did not need to hide your flaws from them. You could also trust them to notice your strengths and challenge you to work hard to do more than you had previously thought possible. They brought out something special in you that helped you overcome a struggle or develop a special skill that you value today. I was blessed to have a high school cross-country running coach, Mr. Vann, who was able to help me build my grit to run farther and faster than I ever thought possible. He would tell me my flaws in my mindset, detect my unreasonable expectations and then inspire me to do better the next time. He insisted that I never make excuses for my failures and refocused me upon what I needed to do in my thinking and training in order to become a nationally ranked runner, something that had never occurred to me when I initially tried out for the team. He was such a compassionate and effective coach that he had the largest turnout of any of the sports teams at my school. He let everyone join the team. He even had teens quitting smoking in order to join the team. He knew that every child had the potential to fit in somewhere on the range of varsity and A through F teams and find their inner distance runner. This is especially amazing when you consider how grueling running distances over hills, valleys and streams can be. Everyone on the team knew that Coach Vann loved us and expected great things from us. He was very clear about his disappointment when we did not train hard, support each other or when we tried to blame others for a disappointing performance. He also had an uncanny eye for each person's personal weak spots in how they approached running and he expected us to each work on our weak points. He made it clear that we each owed ourselves and our team mates a willingness to work hard and take responsibility for making forward progress. He repeatedly told us that winning did not matter unless we knew that we had trained properly, run our races well and supported everyone on the team. He even berated the entire team when we won a tournament by being lazy and taking advantage of not having any of our major competitors present by running slow and sloppy races. At this same tournament, he made a good example of one of our slowest runners who was the only one to run a personal best when the rest of us ran like we were on vacation. He made it clear that the slowest members of each team were also just as important as the fastest runners because the entire team's times and places were added together to determine the winning team. He also repeatedly drew our attention to the value of our personal character outside of sport and drew parallels with future challenges we would face in life. The net effect of his coaching was that our team became the state champion for both boys and girls even though none of us had any prior experience with distance running (because at that time in history there was no such thing as distance running programs for children prior to high school). Coach Vann is the kind of man who I wish every child could experience because of his ability to be compassionate, patient and demanding at the same time.

HOT TIP

Parents who realize that their job is to cultivate good character and grit in their children have the advantage over parents who believe they are supposed to help their kids perform well.

This attitude of kind, nonjudgmental observation and empathy coupled with clear-eyed encouragement in the struggle toward greatness is compassion. Compassion sees both the child who is and the person the child can become according to that child's strengths and limitations. Compassion serves for the benefit of the other without any assumption of self-gain. It is willing to be sacrificial. It is not clouded by expectations that do not fit the child. Compassion is free of the need for self-gratification and this is where some parents fail.

Many parents who see me confuse a desire for the best for their child with compassion. Your deep love for your child may not always be compassionate. For example, if you believe that your child must attend a prestigious school or play sports on a prestigious team in order to develop good self-esteem and get ahead in life, then you are not being compassionate, unless they happen to be a naturally gifted thespian or athlete in the making. Pushing your child to be the best at something when this is not their natural area of strength accidentally teaches your child to assume that competing with and beating others is what leads to joy and long-term success. It gives an accidental message of shame and failure for not being really talented, for not being better than others or for not earning awards. For example, when you think of a really good school, don't you automatically think about the number of awards the children of that school have won, the number of children who became famous who once attended that school or the statistics that show the children of that school get much better scores than those of other schools? How compassionate is it to live as though being special and being the best is what matters? The irony is that I hear almost all of the parents I see tell me that their child needs the best in care and extracurriculars and that they are also especially bright and talented when it could not possibly be true. I know that statistically speaking, that child is going to be average, earn an average income, have an average number of divorces and have an average number of children by the time they are forty, no matter who they might be. Doesn't the concept of compassion dictate that we love our children for who they are rather than for who we wish they would be?

Cultivating compassion for your child's experience of living with an anxiety disorder also mandates that you teach your child how to redirect their fight/flight or freeze response by learning to ignore it and proceed as though it never happened. It means that you will see the big picture for your child's life and understand that you need to help your child build competence under duress instead of dependence upon you. You might be forgetting that every child needs to learn how to live well despite experiencing distressing emotions and thoughts. Every child needs to realize that they can build the ability to persevere under duress if they practice and that this gritty ability to persevere will bring much joy and long-term success. When you repeatedly swoop in to stop tears and distress in your child, you might be feeling competent and powerful in your ability to soothe your child, which gratifies you; however, you are also preventing your child from learning to soothe themselves, which is an essential emotional life skill. You are accidentally sculpting your child's mind to believe that only an authority can handle their distress. Compassion is much more far-sighted than momentary relief of suffering. Compassion sees both the present and the future and understands what will benefit the child over the full course of their life.

PARENT RESILIENCY RULE 7

Use the power of your love to push necessary growth for the sake of your child's future joy by ignoring the urge to make life easy for them in the present.

What is it about compassion that is so powerful for human growth and emotional development? Kristen Neff (Neff *et al.*, 2018) and many others have done some exciting research that shows that learning to view others and oneself with compassion gives people a psychological edge when managing difficult situations, such as having an anxiety disorder. Children, teens and parents who learn to be compassionate toward themselves and others are quicker to recover from mistakes, stressors and traumas than those who lack this skill, especially when they are perfectionistic (Warren, Smeets & Neff, 2016). People who are compassionate also have enhanced immune functioning and better health. They also recover from anxiety disorders and depression more readily and have fewer relapses (Neff, 2012). Developing compassion for yourself and your child, therefore, is going to power up your parenting and improve your child's inner felt experience of being a kid who has an anxiety disorder.

What is compassion?

Compassion is your ability to view yourself or your child with kindness, empathy, and tolerance while free from any expectation of return to yourself. Empathy is your ability to accurately detect the emotions another person is experiencing. Compassion means you put aside any expectations you might have about how your child treats you or feels about you and instead simply assume that whatever your child is experiencing is there for a good reason that makes sense to your child, even if you do not understand or do not agree with your child's mindset. There is no disappointment, no anger at things missed or frustration with rudeness or disrespect. There is no regret, just a loving kind emotional embracing of your child at that moment. Compassion means that your actions and feelings are directed for the sake of your child without expectation of something in return, such as recognition for your efforts or desire for a return of a favor. It entails an accurate understanding of your child's true needs (as opposed to their wants) and makes no assumptions. It is the opposite of quid pro quo. Does this sound familiar to you? It is the same thing that Christians call *agape*, a Greek word that means a selfless love of others that places their needs equal to or above your own. If you have practiced yoga or meditation, you might have encountered this concept during lovingkindness meditation. It means putting your emotional baggage aside for the sake of loving yourself or, in this case, your child.

Speaking as a parent and professional, I realize that compassion needs to become a practice for all parents and also requires self-compassion for the myriad of times we all fail at being compassionate. That is part of compassion. It allows you to forgive yourself and your child for their moments of humanity that are irksome, foolish or immoral. For example, my youngest son has a long history of anxiety, starting with selective mutism, then social anxiety disorder, then obsessive compulsive disorder and lastly bipolar disorder. He also has some learning disabilities. His older brother, as I mentioned earlier, has some substantial disabilities and an alphabet soup of diagnoses. When I got pregnant with my second child, I had hopes that he would be spared any diagnoses that required intervention or special education. My reaction to the news of his early challenges with anxiety was much calmer than how I felt when I encountered his older brother's challenges. I was calm and accepting about anxiety disorders and learning disabilities because by then I knew that family genetics would make that a likelihood. I did not feel heroic or dismayed, just resolute about the task of raising him.

When he attempted suicide, however, I was resentful and scared, because I did not yet realize he had bipolar disorder. I had assumed that fate owed me a free pass on serious life-threatening mental illness. I admit that I felt furious at being in the situation of fearing for my son's life, so terrified that I was angry because he attempted to kill himself and had such little regard for his life that was precious to me. I also felt angry that I had yet another mental health thing to deal with when his step-siblings seemed unscathed by any mental health dilemmas. I also felt shame that I had this response because I knew it was irrational. I was embarrassed that I was the mental health professional whose birth children were mental health hot messes and not likely to be voted the kid you most want to adopt. I knew that my son's bipolar disorder was not of anyone's doing but I still felt cheated and angry for both of us. I had hoped for a son who was easier to raise and easy for others to praise.

I had two choices for handling my reaction to my son's situation. I could continue to feel full of shame, embarrassment and resentment or I could work on my self-compassion and compassion for my son. I chose to work on compassion since it felt absolutely miserable to be full of resentment, shame and feeling betrayed by fate. Here is how I did it. First, I talked to my most trusted kind friends and told them exactly how nonheroic, ashamed, resentful and scared I felt. I allowed them to give me their love and kindness and to show me that they did not think poorly of me for feeling this way. They did not expect me to be heroic or graceful about racing home from work every day to visit my son in the inpatient unit. They did not expect me to be anything other than a human being who was reacting to a difficult situation that hurt, even though I was very practiced at being a parent of a complicated child and practiced at working with children who had serious mental health conditions. They spoke words of kindness to me. They helped me recognize when I was expecting too much of myself or of my son. This in turn made it easier for me to say kind things to myself and to believe them. It made it easier for me to come to a place of acceptance and gratitude for all that was my son.

My inner dialogue of compassion went something like this: "Of course you are angry and resentful. Most of your patients and their families are indeed less complicated than your kids. Of course, you wish for something to be easier and for your son to be spared suffering. No parent wants their child to have any mental illness or to try to kill themselves. You cannot control some of the things that are going on with your son no matter how much you wish you could. You are only human. So is your son. Of course, you wish that your parenting could have been so good your son did not have all these problems, but no human parent can achieve that. You have done your best and tried your hardest. This is just difficult and painful. You are not alone. Many families live the same kind of life you are living. Just because you have special knowledge does not protect your children from genetics or the influence of the environment. You are allowed to feel sad, angry, hurt or whatever. That does not make you a bad parent or a bad Christian. It just makes you human. You are loved by God who sees all and understands all. Your husband, God and friends are here with you on this journey and they share your pain and will share the burden. They will all help you figure out how to help your son manage his burdens. Your kids are also really cool people whom you like and who each have their own version of greatness. They are never boring or uninteresting and you love that about them. This is just the package that they happen to come in. Their struggles make them who they are. They wouldn't be the sons you love if they did not have their complications."

Taking this compassionate stance did not change the situation. It did, however, profoundly change my attitude so I could accept the situation and better show my son the loving acceptance and optimism that he needed from me. I realized that he was scared, regretful and worried about his future too. He was horrified at what he had done and how out of control he had gotten without realizing it. He needed me to be strong in a way that demonstrated calm, kind acceptance and commitment to the uncertain journey of managing bipolar disorder. He needed me to show him that he was still lovable, fun, interesting and himself despite his mental health challenges. Compassion was the only way I could get to this place of grace and acceptance.

Compassion is considered by many practicing Buddhists to be the most important of the virtues. When I volunteered in Bhutan, the elders were the ones who were given the task to make prayers and offerings for compassion for all people and all beings because these were the most important prayers. Retired elders were expected to spend their days making prayers and offerings for compassion. Compassion meditations are considered to be the more advanced and challenging of meditative practices by many Buddhist monks and lamas. This is the opposite of what many western cultures do. Many western cultures just assume that most people have the capacity to be loving and moral and therefore do not reserve their highest efforts to the contemplation and expression of compassion. Individual rights and winning are placed on a higher plane and more attention is given to obtaining justice, enforcing personal rights and being famous or the best than to acts of compassion. This focus on obtaining individual happiness and success, compared to others, and focus upon obtaining individual justice therefore accidentally pushes parents to feel violated when their children are difficult, or to feel envious when other people's children seem to be so much easier and admirable. I am sure that part of Bhutan's claim to be the nation that produces "Gross National Happiness" is partly dependent upon their emphasis on cultivating a life of humble compassion toward every person and being. The highest compliment that can be given to someone in Bhutan is that they are humble and compassionate. Compare this to what gets written in blogs, newspapers and magazines when someone is being admired in western culture.

> **PARENT RESILIENCY RULE 8**
> Cultivate humble compassion toward yourself and your child rather than expertise and success.

The attribution bias

Everyone has a default setting for how to explain others' behavior to themselves that needs to be changed. It is called the *attribution bias*. The attribution bias states that when we make mistakes, we tend to explain our behavior according to the circumstances. For example, when I am late to work, I tell everyone how the traffic was bad and how all the stoplights were working against me. When we explain other people's behavior, however, we tend to explain it according to their bad character. For example, if someone is late to meet you at the coffee shop, then you are likely to think, "They are so disorganized and don't respect other people's time. What's wrong with them?!" The problem with the attribution bias is that it causes us to vilify other people and decreases our ability to feel compassion when they make mistakes. It pushes us away from a compassionate worldview. It is a default setting that sets us up for dissatisfaction and unhappiness with others. The attribution bias also states that when you make a mistake, you explain it according to circumstance so you can maintain a good view of yourself. So, when you are late to a meeting with a friend at the coffee shop, you tell yourself and your friend, "The train was really late today. I cannot believe how long we had to wait when we stopped." The only exception to the attribution bias is when someone has major depression, then they tend to assume that any disappointment that occurs is to be blamed on their own bad character.

The opposite of the attribution bias is to take a compassionate approach in which you explain everyone's behavior, not just your own, according to circumstances. What scientists now understand is that using circumstances to explain everyone's behavior improves our relationships and makes it easier to build healthy relationships. It also leads to feeling happier and feeling more content (Allen, Barton & Stevenson, 2015). Learning to let others off of the hook of unreasonable expectations by assuming that they always have a good reason for what they do makes it easier for us to forgive annoyances, avoid misinterpretation of intentions and develop a mutually agreeable way to handle conflict. Think of it. How do you feel about cooperating with someone who thinks you are lazy, foolish, idiotic or selfish every time you have a rough moment? Whether or not you say your critical thoughts aloud does not diminish its impact on your child. They feel your disapproval and tension and know full well that you are unhappy with them. Simply saying the phrase "It's your behavior that I do not love. I still love you," is not very convincing when you are lacking compassion inside your heart. It is about as good as my children's venomous "I'm sorry" when forced to apologize to the sibling they just pummeled. You cannot hide your disappointment, resentment or worry from your child no matter how often you say "I love you." Using compassion to offset the attribution bias will help your statements of love acquire weight and meaning for your child because it will make your words, actions and feelings match one another.

HOT TIP

Learn to assume that your child's behavior is always the product of circumstances that need to be understood in order to help them mature.

Cultivating compassion

You need to approach cultivating compassion as a daily practice of improving your ability to imagine and express selfless kindness, tolerance, forgiveness and generosity toward yourself and your family. You also need to realize that all parents need to work on their self-compassion and compassion toward their offspring. It is very possible to love your child completely yet be lacking in compassion. It is nothing to be ashamed of when you experience a compassion fail. It is just part of being a parent. Compassion is not something you do by just making up your mind to be kind. You have to be willing to repeatedly catch and correct yourself when your compassion fails and then do it again and again until it becomes a habit. This means that you will need to repeatedly find ways to remind yourself of your need to improve your self-compassion and your compassion toward your anxious child. Let's start by identifying how you know when you are off track and experiencing a compassion fail. Here is a list of typical indicators that your compassion skills are lacking:

- You lose your temper with yourself or your child.

- You mutter under your breath about your child.

- You mentally refer to yourself or your child in critical or contemptuous terms, e.g., how stupid, how idiotic, wouldn't you know, I am such a horrible mum, or using swear words.

- You feel ashamed of your child and/or yourself.

- You wish you or your child were someone else.

- You feel hatred, disgust or resentment toward yourself or your child.

- You dread the next encounter with your child or their anxiety.

- You feel disappointed or ashamed of your child because of their anxiety and inability to get over it as quickly or thoroughly as you think they should.

- You feel impatient with your child's ability to manage their anxiety.

- You resent your partner for the way they handle your child's anxiety.

- You wish you could send your child to a long-term boarding school or remote desert island to let someone else deal with their anxiety.

- You blame your child for ruining your vacation, your marriage/relationship or your life.

> **HOT TIP**
>
> Compassion is not something you do by just making up your mind to be kind. You have to be willing to repeatedly catch yourself and correct yourself when your compassion fails until it becomes a habit.

Once you recognize that you have accidentally had a compassion fail, you can attempt any of the following exercises to help get yourself back on track. First, we will start with self-compassion so you can get yourself back into a productive parenting mode. It will be much easier to feel and express compassion toward your child if you first give some to yourself. Please be aware that many parents get teary-eyed or cry when they write these letters because they so desperately need to see and hear these words of compassion.

1. Write a letter to yourself from the perspective of the most loving person or being you know. If you had a parent, grandparent, teacher, coach or mentor who embodied compassion, write as though they are seeing all of you and giving you their kindness and encouragement. If you cannot think of a person you have known, you can pick someone from literature or the media, such as author and inspirational speaker Brené Brown. If your view of God is as a perfectly loving being, then you can write from the perspective of God looking at you with perfect compassion. I had one patient who

COMPASSION AND THE NEW NORMAL

used her golden retriever dog as the one who wrote her a compassionate letter because her dog embodied perfect love, forgiveness and acceptance. When you write the letter, have your compassionate person address you in a kind manner and describe what they see inside of you, how you feel, how much you are hurting about what you cannot control or make better, what they wish you understood about yourself that you are not able to see and how they see your good intentions and hurt about failure to make things better. Have this person tell you how much they love you, care for you and are standing with you in your struggles. Have them tell you what they wish you could understand about yourself and your situation so you would not be so hard on yourself.

2. Place a chair in front of you and pretend that you are sitting in that chair. Speak aloud the words of compassion to yourself from the perspective of the most compassionate person, deity or being you know. Address yourself in a kind manner and describe what you see inside of yourself sitting in the chair in front of you. Tell yourself about all of the pain you are feeling about what you cannot control or make better, about what you wish you understood. Describe all good intentions you see in yourself and how these good intentions have been hurt by a failure to make things better. Tell yourself how much you love yourself, how much you care and how you will stand by yourself throughout your struggles. Tell yourself what you wish you could understand about yourself and your situation so you will not be so hard on yourself. You can also do this by reading the letter aloud that you wrote in Exercise 1.

3. This one is for pet owners who have an affectionate relationship with their pet. Pretend your pet can speak aloud how they feel about you and how they see you as the one worthy of an enthusiastic welcome every time they see you. Write down what your pet would tell you to think and feel about the situation that distresses you when they see you walk in the door. Have your pet tell you what they think you should notice and focus upon. Have them express their love and gratitude for your presence and good intentions. Have them tell you how they accept and love you even when you fail to be perfect and how they will always stick by your side.

4. Each time you find yourself using critical words toward yourself, stop and replace these words with the phrase "I am doing the best I can with what I have." Make this phrase a habit of thought when you feel disappointed in yourself, when you feel embarrassed or when you feel like a failure. This phrase is very helpful because it acknowledges that no one intends to fail at living and that everyone reflects their unique circumstances in how they think, act and react.

PARENT RESILIENCY RULE 9

Assume that you, your child and everyone else are doing the best they can with what they have. Memorize this phrase: "I am doing the best that I can with what I have." Make it your automatic response when you feel disappointed in yourself. When you are disappointed with others, memorize this phrase and say to yourself, "They are doing the best they can with what they have."

COMPASSION EXERCISES TO HELP YOU GIVE COMPASSION TO YOUR CHILD

1. Imagine that you are the perfectly kind and loving person, deity or pet that you admire. Write down what this being would say to your child about the situation that provoked you. Have them address your child in a kind and loving manner, "My Dear Child," or "My Precious _____." Have this being tell your child about the hurt and frustration felt by your child, "I see that you are so sad and angry that you did another compulsion in front of your best friend. I know you feel humiliated and wish that you did not have to deal with so much anxiety." Have your compassionate being, or person, tell your child about the good intentions you see, the areas of limitation caused by anxiety and the better person you see them becoming. "I know you wish you could just get rid of your obsessive-compulsive disorder (OCD) and that you would never do any compulsions or avoidance if you had your way. You feel so bullied and controlled by your OCD." Tell them how much you love them and will stand by them. "I love you and your OCD will never change that. I am here to stand by you and remind you that I love you no matter what." Comfort your child by showing them that you stand with them in their pain, their struggle and that you love them regardless of their symptoms or progress in therapy. "I wish you knew what a great kid you are and that I am here for you no matter what happens with your OCD. I want you to feel loved and know that step by step we are going to get through this together. You are still a wonderful person."

2. Now, go tell your child or write your child what you generated in the previous exercise. Say aloud, or write down and read, your statement of compassion. You might need to practice first until you get comfortable talking to your child in this manner without giving any advice, without correcting them or trying to persuade them to do their therapy home practice.

COMPASSION EXERCISES TO HELP YOUR CHILD LEARN COMPASSION

1. Start trying to talk to your child in a compassionate manner whenever you feel the urge to lose your temper or get stuck in advice giving. Do this before tucking them in at nighttime or before they leave for school. Make sure they hear words of compassion every time they complain about their anxiety or want to give up trying to overcome their anxiety. Make this your default response when they get stuck due to anxiety.

    Example: "Looks like today was really rough for you because of your anxiety. I know that you wish you didn't have to deal with anxiety and desperately want this to be behind you. I see what a great kid you are, how kind you are to the cat and how good humored you are with your best friend. I know that someday you will be much stronger and capable at overcoming your anxiety until it won't be such a big problem. I love you and am here with you while you are learning how to tackle anxiety and I am glad to help you in any way that I can. Someday I know you will be proud of how you overcome your anxiety."

2. When you make a mistake, speak aloud in front of your child or teen by saying, "I am just doing the best I can with what I have. Some days are more frustrating than others." Be a role model of how to think and react to frustration, disappointment and failure. Our children

learn much more by watching us go about our daily activities than they do by hearing an inspirational speech. When others make mistakes, delete critical comments. For example, when someone cuts in front of you in traffic, say, "They must really be in a hurry," instead of saying, "***#%@" or "That idiot!"

3. Start asking your child to take a compassionate perspective about their situation whenever you hear self-criticism or self-contempt. Your goal is not to help them solve their problem. It is to help them kindly view themselves as a human being who is struggling with the circumstance of being sucker punched by anxiety.

Example: If your child refuses to take their medication and says this: "I hate going to therapy. I hate my life! I am so sick of taking pills and having to talk to therapists and doctors," then you should say, "I can see how frustrating it must be to have to do all these things to get over your anxiety. I see how you feel so alone and singled out because of all your treatment. I wish you could feel how proud I am of how you keep on going with school, treatment and keeping up with your friends even though your anxiety makes you miserable. I wish you could see your future when you have this behind you and realize how strong you are. I know it is really difficult. I am here with you every step of the way especially when you stumble and want to give up. I love you whether or not you like therapy or your pills. I see how you are much more than your anxiety even when it seems overwhelming. Here, let's take your meds and face this thing together."

Example: If your younger child who has social anxiety says, "No one likes me. I never get asked to play by the other kids. I don't want to leave the house!" you can say, "I see how much your anxiety hurts you by making you feel like no one likes you. It is so hard to have to listen to those scary thoughts that make you feel like giving up and playing alone. Any kid who has anxiety that tries to convince them that no one wants to play with them would have a hard time leaving the house. I wish you could see how cool I see you are and how much other kids would enjoy you if you could play with them without feeling so embarrassed or anxious. I love you no matter how much your anxiety bothers you and makes it hard to want to do things. I know that someday you will get past your anxiety and be the kid that I know you wish you could be with good friends who like playing with you. Let's get your backpack and leave for school."

4. When your child, teen or young adult expresses self-criticism and disgust, help them reframe their self-critical thoughts by asking them open ended questions that direct them to take a kind perspective. Here are some great questions to ask:

   a. If you had a best friend who felt like you and had your anxiety, what would you say to them? What would happen if you said this same thing to yourself?

   b. If God, your pet, your grandmother or other known kind being could talk to you right now, what would he/she/they say? What would happen to you if you talked to yourself like they would?

c. What would happen if you said to yourself, "I don't like having anxiety right now and it really frustrates me," instead of "I am such an idiot!"

d. How would you feel about being you if you told yourself, "I am doing the best I can with what I have?" instead of "I am such a failure!"

e. Does calling yourself a name help you cope better? What would happen if you just described how you felt and left out the name calling?

Next, we will work on improving your and your child's ability to appreciate imperfection and the lessons learned from struggling with anxiety. It will be a way to help you and your child develop hope and a healthy perspective about living with anxiety.

— CHAPTER 5 —

The Value of Imperfection

We live in a culture that idealizes a narrow definition of success. This narrow standard of success includes many things that look good on social media, seem appealing and seem to offer a guarantee of escaping many of life's problems. When I ask parents what they want for their children, they almost always tell me, "I just want them to be happy. I also want them to go to a good college, so they get a good job." When I ask what makes going to a good college so advantageous for getting a good job, they tell me that this means that their child will become part of an elite group of peers and professors who will launch them into a good career. This sounds reasonable, right? This is in contrast to what my grandparents expected of my parents. My two sets of grandparents each expected my parents to do things that served others and enacted their Christian faith, guaranteed they moved out and supported themselves. They were also not supposed to complain about their job if it paid the bills. No one was worrying about happiness and it was assumed that any job that helped you pay your bills was a good one.

If you look under the surface of these expectations that

most parents have today, you see that the shift has turned toward raising children who feel pleased with life, themselves and their work. When I ask parents to define what "good" means in reference to education and jobs, they often reply with something that refers to schools and jobs that others recognize as being prestigious and well-paid. They often tend to assume that white collar professional jobs are somehow better than other jobs and careers that require a graduate education are preferable because they presage obtaining a white collar job. This change in aspirations for children and teens is also reflected in the aspirations of children. When twenty-first-century children are asked what they want to be when they grow up, without suggesting a list of possible careers or jobs, more than 70 percent say they want to be a YouTube star, rich or a rock star (Berger *et al.*, 2019). Thirty years ago, children and teens who answered the same question did so by listing various jobs and family roles, such as becoming a teacher, a doctor, a mechanic, a mother or a father. The aspirations of youth reflect the subtle and not so subtle pressure from their families and the culture to become a person who is remarkable, has unlimited resources and earns the admiration of everyone. We also see that the careers they see portrayed on digital media greatly influence their choices for their aspirations. In stark contradiction to these aspirational goals and the attempts of parents to raise happy children, the rate of anxiety disorders, mood disorders, suicide attempts and suicide completions has risen in the population of children born after 1990 (Auerbach *et al.*, 2018). What has gone wrong? What's wrong with wanting the best for your child? Isn't that what all parents should want?

For starters, how do you determine what "the best" is? How does a child know when they are "the best" or living "the best" life? You either have to use the criteria of always being in first place, always beating out others and always gaining the admiration of others, or you have to use markers of fame, such as the number of followers or likes you accumulate on your social media. You accidentally become the victim of the approval of other people. You end up needing external praise, awards and acknowledgments in order to determine if you are acceptable and living the best way possible. Can you see the trap that this creates for your young children? You end up focusing upon striving to perform in order to gain approval and you overlook developing your own internal standards for success and good character. You end up eternally chasing after others to get their good words of approval and become over sensitized to corrective feedback and disapproval. I see this all too often amongst my patients and their families. The pursuit of "the best" becomes a never good enough attempt to just get through the next step of success with no end point in sight. It also means that your child will have a bad day whenever they make mistakes, encounter someone who is not forthcoming with praise or enter into situations in which others are more accomplished. Research on resilience and getting gritty about overcoming problems such as anxiety shows that the better approach toward life is to view challenges as opportunities to improve skills and develop competence instead of opportunities to win (McGonigal, 2015). This approach helps your child learn to appreciate the process of growing, recovering from mistakes and learning from mistakes instead of always aiming to be the best at any moment. Learning to enjoy the act of mastery is a valuable life skill for your child who suffers from anxiety because it will give them the ability to repeatedly face their symptoms with courage and tenacity whenever they recur.

What's wrong with wanting to be happy?

Setting the expectation that one should achieve happiness, rather than competency, sets your child up for disappointment. Surveys of college-age adults show that they believe that they are supposed to be happy (Busby, 2018). Yet, research on their mental health shows that they are actually less happy than previous generations, even though their happiness has been a stated goal for their upbringing. Research also shows that children now believe that stress is a negative thing and something that requires special recovery time. What has gone wrong? Kelly McGonigal's research (McGonigal, 2015) on stress reveals that stress itself is not detrimental to physical or mental health. *It is the attitude about stress that make the experience of stress detrimental.* Individuals who believe that stress is a challenge to be overcome or that will serve as an opportunity for growth get emotionally stronger when they encounter stressors. Your children will improve their resilience when they encounter stress if they believe that stress will make them stronger and more capable. Your children need to assume that stress is inevitable and a normal part of life, as opposed to being something to be avoided or that requires special efforts at recovery.

If your child believes that they should be happy, then it causes them to misinterpret the presence of distress and unhappiness as a personal failure or as something bad that should be avoided. This shows up in the attitude that I see amongst many children and their parents in which they believe they need mental health days off from school to recover from taking exams or quizzes or after applying to colleges because they view these events as being terribly significant, difficult, distressing and dangerously stressful. Your child would benefit greatly if they viewed quizzes, tests and college entrance applications as a normal part of going to school and growing up. I have had many patients' parents inform me that they called their child in sick the day after exams or after filling out college applications "because they need a mental health day or a stress break." I have even had the irony of parents calling to cancel a therapy session so they could give their child a "mental health break!" If you accidentally do this in a misguided attempt to help your child cope with stress, you undermine your child's ability to grow strong in their mental health. Sometimes part of learning to live with joy means learning to be tolerant and low key about feeling unpleasant while doing difficult things.

For example, many seemingly successful kids and parents I see in my practice falsely believe that when they are placed in a schoolwork group with someone they dislike, the teacher should re-sort the groups in order to situate their child with only preferred peers. The same thing can happen when a child is placed with a teacher they dislike as opposed to being placed in the popular teacher's class. The parents act as though it is terrible for their child to encounter daily frustration, such as having to spend time around people they dislike. They falsely believe that their child needs special consideration because they have an anxiety disorder. When the teacher or head of school denies the request, then the child and parents become very upset and feel as though the entire school year has been lost. They mistakenly assume that the reason the child is anxious or depressed must be due to having a "bad" placement, as opposed to realizing that every child, even an anxious one, needs to learn how to thrive when life presents frustration and disappointment.

> ### HOT TIP
> Your child's greatest opportunity to develop resilience and the ability to recover quickly from stress is when they have to repeatedly face disappointing and frustrating situations.

What is the advantage to your child in encountering the dilemmas of living in an imperfect world that cannot be made better or easier? They will have the opportunity to learn how to thrive when they encounter the unexpected or the challenging. These situations teach your child how to become effective by refocusing upon what they can control, regardless of the situation. Your child learns that ultimately the only thing possible to control is their own attitude and behavior and that this can be powerful in achieving their goals when things get rough. Having frequent encounters with less than ideal situations also prepares your child for the inevitable future life they will lead when some of their bosses, supervisors, professors or workmates will inevitably not be to their liking. It prepares them to succeed and be productive when life has its rough and unpleasant moments. Being able to tolerate people who are less than your best friend is a very important skill for someone who wants to live well, experience joy, maintain employment and raise a family. Be honest, how many times has your work group, sports team or volunteer group been filled with all of your favorite people who always do their bit really well with a pleasant expression on their face? Don't you have to encounter difficult people and disappointment on a regular basis? Do you really want these encounters to cost you a lot of emotional energy and recovery time? In my home, my husband and I know that the only one who is always easy to get along with is the family dog. That means we try to be low key about all of the other encounters that might be less than lovely in order to feel full of joy and good humor.

This expectation of current and future happiness also impairs parents of anxious children, perhaps like you. When you believe that your child should be happy and easier to raise than what you are currently experiencing, you accidentally risk evaluating your parenting and home life as being a failure. You increase the likelihood that you will panic, worry and get depressed just because your child exhibits symptoms of anxiety and unhappiness. Your child notices your reaction to their distress and then comes to the same faulty conclusion, "Something must be terribly wrong!" They react to your unnecessary distress and get entangled with your faulty assumption that something really is terribly wrong instead of realizing that they need to get on with the task of learning how to manage their anxiety or how to manage an unpleasant situation. They become more distressed and less capable of effective coping.

Research suggests that if you are a parent of a child with an anxiety disorder, then you are more likely to be perfectionistic (Robinson, 2020). Perfectionism occurs when someone has an overly narrow definition of what the right or good thing to do might be and an overemphasis on the significance of mistakes. Many researchers who study the phenomenon of unexpected suicide in highly successful teens and young adults suspect that this pattern of the expectation of happiness and the pressure to achieve overly narrow goals and the pressure to avoid mistakes is behind the unfortunate phenomenon of increasing poor mental health and suicide attempts and completions in the millennial and younger population (Smith *et al.*, 2018).

Let me give you another example to help illustrate what happens when you accidentally believe that your ultimate parenting goal is to help your child achieve happiness. Recently I worked with a preteen who had symptoms of social anxiety disorder and depression. His parents were understandably worried because he had become terribly isolated once the COVID-19 pandemic happened and he was no longer attending school in person. He had two friends he had played with since kindergarten but had lost touch with these two friends because "they had been really mean to our son." I asked the boy and his parents what had happened. They explained that they had been out shopping and run into the two friends who were out together having fun. Obviously, they had not invited my patient to join them. The two boys were friendly, said hello and said things that made it sound like they had been playing together frequently in person during the pandemic quarantine. Both the parents and the patient were offended because they assumed that the patient was no longer considered a friend of these two boys. The parents talked about this event as though it meant that these boys were mean. They had obviously had previous talks with their son about the other boys being mean to their son. The parents were especially angry at the parents of the other boys because they had not made the two friends include their son in their play. They assumed that because the parents of the two friends knew about their son's social anxiety and how difficult it was for their son to make social invitations, that these parents would make sure their son was included in any social activities. The parents explained to me that their son would respond to requests for get-togethers but was not yet able to ask others to join him, unless his parents made the invitation and arranged the get-together. Discussion revealed that these two boys lived in close proximity to each other and the patient lived farther away. These two boys were comfortable inviting peers to hang out, unlike my patient. My patient and his parents reacted to this situation with the same level of ire had these two boys kicked my patient in the shin and called him names. One parent referred to the friendly greeting by the two boys as being "traumatic" as opposed to friendly.

So, what is your reaction to this scenario? Are you siding with the parents of the patient who believed that others should accommodate their son to make him happier and that the two families in question are being unkind or mean? Or do you see how the two boys were still being friendly to my patient and by happenstance were able to play outside together without having to get a parent to drive them to a gathering, such as they would have to do with my patient? Do you accept that living close to each other is grounds for easy friendship and easy get-togethers without being spiteful to the child who lives farther away and who cannot yet call on his own to tell other kids he wants to play? Do you accept that a certain amount of disappointment and unhappiness is just inevitable and not a bad thing? Do you accept that, even though it is disappointing to be left out of play, it is ordinary and something your child must learn not to take personally?

What would have happened had the parents of my patient been able to avoid making the mistake of the attribution bias and instead attributed the friends playing together as being due to lucky circumstance. What would the effect be on their son had they encouraged their son to set up a playdate when the two boys were greeting him with such enthusiasm?

They should have treated the situation as a normal part of life and offered an explanation to their son that validated his distress and also showed that no harm was intended by the two friends. A simple statement of "How wonderful to see Peter and John! They looked like they really missed seeing you. They are lucky they live so close to each other. How about you text them to see when you can get together?" would have done much better. If their son complained about being left out, then they could have told him "They live near each other. Of course, they are going to play together. That does not mean that they do not like you. Look how happy they were to see you. Do you really believe they were faking it? They may not know that you want to get together because you haven't texted them or talked to them since the pandemic started. Let's see if you can reach them now."

Act like distress is a normal part of life

If focusing upon success, being the best, avoiding distress and being happy is unhelpful, then what should you aim for as a parent? The solution is straightforward and simple. Act and talk as though distress and disappointment are just as normal as feeling happy is normal. Act as though all of the emotions are normal and desirable because they are signals of our reaction to our inner beliefs, thoughts and assessment of the situation. Emotions are valuable information that gives your child cues for coping and decision making. Emotions are also ephemeral. They will always fluctuate. When something pleasurable happens, it feels best when we are first aware of the sensation. Our human brain and body get used to all emotions once they occur, just as we get used to any sensation. For example, the first taste of a piece of your favorite treat is intense but dulls as you take repeated bites of the treat. Your body and mind get used to every sensation whether it is pleasant or unpleasant. This is why you cannot hang onto a wonderful moment and also why all painful moments will diminish and pass. Thus, you should treat your child's painful emotions as being signals for coping and adaptation. The goal is not to avoid unpleasant emotions, but rather to assume that your child will repeatedly experience them and needs to develop competence at managing them.

People who handle disappointment well realize that good things can come out of unexpected outcomes. They easily recall times when the unexpected disappointment led to something wonderful. I can recall going backpacking in the mountains with friends, only to have it snow three inches. I was cold and disappointed that my feet and hands might never feel warm for the rest of the trip. I got frostbite which made my toes hurt even worse. I had told myself for years that I would never deliberately go ice camping because it seemed like a miserable thing to do, yet there I was stuck in the middle of an unexpected Spring snowstorm with cold hands and feet and lots and lots of ice. I ended up being surprised by all of the beautiful snow and ice formations in the waterfalls and on the mountains that took my breath away. I felt awe and a deep sense of privilege to have seen these magnificent formations. Each time I recall the beautiful scenes that I saw, I am glad that I endured frostbite and constant cold. I learned that sometimes being really cold is wonderful when you get to personally witness the kind of scenery you otherwise would only see in a winning nature photography portfolio.

Another example is from a patient of mine who had tried out for a competitive position on one of her school's sports teams. It was in a sport that she had participated in since age three and really enjoyed. She did not make the team her first year in high school and her family was worried and disappointed, fearing that she would have difficulty finding a friend group in high school if she did not have a special group to join. They thought that if she made the sports team, then it would give her four years of companionship, self-esteem from being on a winning team and a helpful entry on her college application. Fortunately, her parents were able to insist that there must be other things that their daughter could do to make friends and spend her time. What my patient did instead of sports was teach herself to play guitar. She began composing songs. She got some other teens together to form a band and they began performing her compositions at local venues for free food and tips from the customers. They got better and even got paid for some performances and collected a small following of people who listened to their YouTube videos. When she went to college, she was able to make money on the side performing for people's parties and weddings, which she enjoyed much more than she would have waiting tables or working in a retail store. She tells everyone that missing the chance to be on the sports team was the best thing that ever happened to her because she discovered her musical self.

PARENT RESILIENCY RULE 10

Reframe your child's struggle to overcome anxiety as their golden opportunity to develop into a capable, strong, resilient human being.

When your child learns to turn disappointment into an opportunity to explore, cultivate patience, accept mistakes and accept failure, it gives them the advantage in life of practicing how to adapt. This is the advantage of growing up with an anxiety disorder. Your child will have to learn mastery over distress, disappointment and being less than perfect, which gives them a huge edge in learning to live well. Kids who learn to face fear and adapt despite difficulties develop resilience and optimism. Their life experience shows them that they can do very difficult things and be persistent when they feel like giving up. Their daily practice in facing their fears teaches them that risks are worth taking and that distress can become manageable. They learn that they are more than their disorder and more than what appears on the outside. They learn that they can have fun and live good lives even though things are difficult or disappointing. They learn to laugh in the midst of fear, and they learn to laugh at themselves. They are less likely to measure themselves according to someone else's idea of what is best and more likely to feel confident about making their own decisions about what matters in their life. When handled well in the ways outlined in this book, your child's struggle can become the valuable opportunity in your child's life that helps them become their better self. So, when you accidentally make life too easy for your child because you believe that it is bad for them to suffer and struggle, you block the formation of their resilient better self.

I hear wonderful stories of resilience won on the battlefield of overcoming anxiety again and again when my young patients grow into late adolescence and young adulthood. They write college essays and blogs and record videos that recount how their early struggles with anxiety made them into a better person who is more compassionate toward the suffering of others, who is grittier about doing difficult things and who has learned to be optimistic and take risks because they know they can overcome mistakes and failures.

Each time one of my former patients sends me one of these essays, or their parents sends me a note letting me now how their formerly anxiety-ridden child is now encouraging others to be resilient during difficult times and doing things that once seemed unimaginable, I rejoice. I rejoice because I know that they learned one of the most precious lessons a human can learn. *Suffering is a normal part of life and it is something that can be overcome when you learn to face life with compassion, resourcefulness and grit.* When your kids learn these important skills early in life, they are much less likely to become discouraged when they encounter the struggles of adulthood.

> **HOT TIP**
> The only way to become resilient is by overcoming personal suffering and mistakes. Your child has to practice overcoming adversity in order to become resilient and prepared for adulthood.

EXERCISES TO HELP YOU AND YOUR CHILD EMBRACE STRUGGLE AND OVERCOME PERFECTIONISM

1. Take a moment to recall a time when you had a struggle in your life and identify what you learned from this experience that is valuable to you. Remind yourself of the initial disappointment or despair that you felt and then what helped you to pick yourself up and make efforts toward overcoming the situation or taking the risk of doing something new. If you had/have an anxiety disorder, this would be especially helpful to focus upon. Share this experience with your child or teen and be honest about the difficulties, the time frame it took for you to recover and how much you value this experience now.

2. Tell your child the stories of your failures and struggles. My children have never asked me about any awards I have won, but they have asked me if anyone broke up with me, if I failed any exams, classes or quizzes and if other children ever teased me or refused to be my friend. Be willing to share your humanity.

3. Be a coach for your child. Remind them of Grantland Rice's famous quotation (he was an American sports reporter in the mid-twentieth century): "When the great scorer comes to write your name, it matters not whether you won or lost, but how you played the game." Refocus your child upon the need to persist, be patient, be kind, be generous and get their schoolwork and chores done, regardless of what their anxiety is telling them on any

given day. Emphasize building character and grit over getting it right or never feeling anxious. Give the highest praise for doing things despite feeling anxious, for being kind and generous with others when anxious, for getting normal chores and work done when anxious, as opposed to having a day with no anxiety.

Example: Your child tells you that they could not sleep the night before an exam and that their anxiety is really bad. Your response should be, "Looks like this is a great day to practice taking your exam and going through your day even though it is not ideal. The more you practice, the easier it will get to take your exams when you are anxious and tired. It is just a test, not the proof of the value of your life."

4. Be a role model. When you are disappointed, start wondering aloud about what can be done to make the most of the moment. Take the "making lemonade out of lemons" approach to busy traffic, no seats on the train and anxiety when you least want it. Speak aloud when you encounter disappointment, distress or anxiety and reframe the situation as one of opportunity for improving your coping. Your child or teen will love hearing you struggle and benefit from your good example of recovering from frustration. They do not want you to be perfect! That intimidates them.

Example: When a friend forgets to bring their part of the meal to a gathering, say to everyone, "Well, we don't need a salad or side dish in order to enjoy each other's company. We will have more time to talk if we are not spending so much time eating and we can share in what it is like for people who cannot always afford unlimited food."

5. If you are still reading to, or with, your kids at bedtime, be sure to read stories in which the main characters face and overcome struggles with being less popular, less skilled, more anxious or more easily intimidated. I believe that Harry in the Harry Potter series by J.K. Rowling is beloved because Harry himself has so many ordinary struggles he must overcome in order to obtain greatness. Encourage your teens to read similar stories and biographies that illustrate greatness of character. Ask them questions about what they saw the main character do in their thinking and behavior that helped them become great. Ask them what they would do if they were in the same situation. Let your child/teen know that they are capable of this too.

6. Watch movies together that illustrate a child/teen's struggle with adversity that they overcome. Ask your child/teen questions about what the main character did to overcome the struggle and what your child/teen would do if they were in the same situation. Ask them what they liked about the main character's ability to persist and overcome.

7. Start admiring aloud people who demonstrate great resilience. Do an online search for celebrities your child/teen might admire who admit that they have

an anxiety disorder and have undergone successful treatment in order to live well. If you have the opportunity to listen to such a person speak, allow your child/teen to hear them and if possible, interact with them. Great examples of people who have overcome great adversity are Lou Zamperini, Helen Keller, Frederick Douglass, Lily Rice, Cornel Hrisca-Munn, Jamie Brewer and Luca Paterelli.

8. Let your child/teen tell their story of coping and overcoming adversity. Every time one of my patients has chosen to do a report or class presentation on their disorder and what it is like to live with their disorder, they have become someone other kids admire for their coping. They have reinforced their belief in their ability to cope and renewed their commitment to living well despite their anxiety disorder. I have seen the same good things happen when a teen or young adult has blogged or made videos about their experience and how they have coped. The focus should be upon coping and overcoming as opposed to complaining about the misery of anxiety in order to be helpful.

9. Have your child conduct experiments in imperfection. Challenge them to hand in some schoolwork with one deliberate mistake to see what happens. How do they feel? Will they remember this when they are in their sixties? Do other people notice? How bad is it really? Have them do the same in sports or the arts. Have them make a holiday decoration that has a least one flaw in it and make sure to display it. Tell your child that they cannot tell anyone about the flaw or apologize for the

flaw and wait to see if anyone notices. You can also have them wear mismatched socks to school or out to play to see what happens. Your goal is to get them to notice that the consequences are quite small and survivable and then forgettable.

CHAPTER 6

Good Humor and Exposure Practice Is Not a Contradiction

When was the last time you and your anxious child had a good laugh about living with anxiety? Or a good laugh during exposure practice (deliberately facing the situations that make your child anxious)? Your answer is bound to be something like the majority of the families I work with, "Not very much, thank you!" You and your child are also very likely to feel serious and less good humored because anxiety pushes you to selectively focus upon negative and frightening ideas. Your, and your child's, sense of humor might have atrophied since the advent of your child's anxiety symptoms. This is a problem because it cuts you and your child off from the mental and physical benefits of good humor. Let me explain.

What is so good about good humor?

Research on good humor, the ability to enjoy the absurdity in yourself and the situation because you recognize that we all are absurd, shows that people who cultivate and enjoy good humor have the mental and physical health advantage over those who lack good humor, especially when under duress. Laughter is powerful. Having a good belly laugh, whether it is spontaneous, or one we induce by listening to a recording of laughter or seeing others laugh, such as in a laughing yoga class, produces the same neurochemical effect that twenty minutes of mindful meditation produces (Eckelkamp, 2014). Laughter gives your brain a quick jolt of dopamine, the feel-good chemical that is associated with getting high, drunk or just happy (Yim, 2016). Laughter also decreases inflammation in your body, which is important for lowering your risk for heart disease, cancer, hypertension and mental illnesses. Laughter also diminishes your experience of physical and mental pain, such as anxiety (Bourg-Carter, 2011). If you listen to a joke, crack a joke or see something funny, you also become more creative when solving problems and perform better on tests because good humor forces you to radically switch perspective and become more flexible in your thinking (Burton, 2020). Furthermore, the good effect of laughter works whether it is a fake laugh or a genuine laugh. We also see that people who are happily married for many years often cite their partner's good humor as being one of the ingredients to their marital success because it helped them weather the difficult times. Do you see the pattern? Learning to switch the gears of your mind from an anxious serious negative pattern into a good-humored one has tremendous benefits.

I should mention that sarcasm is not good humor. Sarcasm is a form of humor that expresses anger and is best enjoyed when a professional comedian is dishing it out. Sarcasm may seem cool when you are in your teens or young adult years, but it has a biting angry edge that creates negative feelings.

Sarcasm is best avoided for the sake of good mental health. So, if you, or your child, prides yourself on your sarcasm, I challenge you to take an honest look at the subtle and not so subtle anger that spreads when you indulge in a sarcastic comment either aloud or inside your own mind. Sarcasm most certainly is not compassionate. You already know from the previous chapter that you want to avoid anything that interferes with the process of compassion.

HOT TIP

Learn to avoid sarcasm in your home because it expresses anger and bitterness and does not create good humor.

When you have an anxious child, your ideal path is to create an exposure-based lifestyle that invites your child to repeatedly practice the things they dread. Exposure-based therapies are the ones that have the most power to help your child recover. They involve directly facing sensations, images, thoughts and situations that your child would rather avoid. Successful exposure therapy requires that your child repeatedly practice all the situations they dread until they get used to it and discover they can manage their anxiety without avoiding, being compulsive, getting reassurance or having a meltdown. It means that you should be funneling your child into acts of exposure without doing anything to quickly make them feel better while they learn that their anxiety subsides on its own. If your child is like the children (and adults!) I see, then they are likely to express their reluctance to do something that seems so preposterous and fear-provoking. My experience has shown me that preteens and teens are the ones most likely to respond with outright anger, refusal or the false claim that they can already do an exposure exercise on their own. This is where your good humor can become invaluable for keeping the atmosphere around treatment positive and forward moving despite your child's fear and grumpiness.

If you are like most parents, you likely respond to your child's anxiety with alarm and the belief that the best solution is the one that eliminates anxiety as rapidly as possible. You might also have been terrorized by your child's tantrums, statements of suicidal intent, or their willingness to say and do extreme things when confronted with exposure practice. While it may generally be a good idea for any parent to pay attention to their child's distress, the quick comforting response that you provide an infant is not appropriate for an older child when they are anxious. As mentioned previously, your child needs a coach who can mentor them in learning how to manage the distress of anxiety. This process begins the first time your young child throws a tantrum and has to adjust to the fact that no one should get everything they want and then continues through emerging adulthood where they repeatedly encounter frustration and disappointment. Learning to take a good-humored approach to the process of your child's maturation by facing their fears makes this process easier and more enjoyable for everyone. It also helps to create the atmosphere that is most advantageous to your child's mental wellness. You and your child can learn that life can be enjoyed even in the midst of struggle and anxiety. Wouldn't you rather be the one who finds the funny in the middle of the chaos than the one who is too serious and rarely cracks a smile?

What is good humor?

First, let's define what is meant by good humor. Good humor is the ability to see the absurdity in yourself, the situation and in others because you realize that the entire human race is often comical in its mistakes, aspirations and unintended outcomes. Good humor is not making fun of others at their expense, but it is enjoying a good belly laugh together when you can both enjoy the silliness of the situation. Good humor embraces the flawed and foolish side of human nature and enjoys it knowing that we are all in the same boat of absurdity together.

Finding the funny in the struggle

Learning to cultivate and improve your family's sense of humor about anxiety can take some work. You have to learn to ignore and turn away from the messages of tragedy that your mind sends your way when you encounter evidence of your child's anxiety disorder. I recall when my youngest son, who was a preteen with social anxiety disorder, began protesting serving as an acolyte at church. Since my church was small, all of the youth were drafted to carry the cross and the long candle tapers in a processional at the beginning and the end of church. My son was feeling the pressure of embarrassment about wearing a white robe and walking down the church aisle while all eyes were upon him. He was also feeling the pressure of his newly developing adolescent perspective that challenged all parental beliefs as being stupid and worthy of rebellion. One Sunday he yelled in the car for the entirety of the ride to church about how he was not going to serve as an acolyte and how dare I, or any other adult, require a self-declared atheist to carry the cross. I explained to him that he needed to be a willing volunteer and do his bit to help the worship service carry on regardless of whether or not he had pleasant feelings about Christianity. When I pushed him out of the car to go get robed up, I hoped with all my heart that he would quiet down and just do his job. When I walked into the church with the rest of my family, I saw my rebel son robed and holding the cross with the other acolytes and the pastor. As soon as he saw me, he yelled out, in an attempt to embarrass and hopefully get himself taken off the acolyte roster, "Mom, this is so hypocritical. You are forcing an atheist to carry the cross!" He yelled it so loudly that every person in the church looked first his way and then my way to see what would happen. My pastor, who has six children and had survived four bouts of adolescence by that time, replied loudly, "That is no problem at all because it is ancient Church tradition. The Romans made Simon of Cyrene carry Jesus' cross on the way to Jesus' crucifixion and he didn't believe in Jesus either!" I and every other parent burst into laughter or big grins which totally defused the situation, including my son's anger. I still laugh when I think about this episode in which a good-humored remark by my pastor prevented an angry anxious kid from blowing up the situation. My pastor's good humor gave my son a good-humored "It's OK to be upset and we are not going to get upset just because you are" response that both defused his tantrum and sent the message that, no matter what, you fulfill your job duties.

PARENT RESILIENCY RULE 11

Prepare yourself with good humor so you can enjoy the moments of embarrassment and absurdity that your child's anxiety will impose.

I also recall the time I was desperately hoping that my family would pass for "normal" and look like all of the other families when we went out into public. Even though I realized that there was no such thing as normal and that almost all families have struggles whether hidden or obvious, I still wanted to see what it was like to have my family be the one who looked like the television version of average. I wanted to feel what it was like to be the family that drew no attention to itself for things that could be chalked up to needing special education or mental health intervention. I was tired of seeing others pity me when my oldest son did things that revealed his cerebral palsy, Tourette's syndrome or ADHD. I wished that my youngest would look people in the eyes, smile at them and respond to their social greetings or go up to other kids who recognized him and greeted him. Seeing them side by side with their step-siblings made these differences more obvious. It was my fantasy to have us all sit in church, look like we were all paying attention, or at least not squabbling with one another, and appear to be clean, tidy and looking like a family with nothing peculiar going on. I just wanted what most of you want, a few moments of others admiring my wonderful kids and not having to feel embarrassed because I was the psychologist parent of "those kids."

I rushed home from work, as did my husband, to gather our four youngest kids and rush to church during Holy Week, the time of the church year in which attendance is high and the services tend to be solemn, serious and deeply meaningful. My job with my oldest son is to make sure he has his clothes on right side out, has his clothing on instead of his seven years' younger brother's clothing, and to make sure that he switches out tops if he has too many food or drool stains on his shirt. This particular time, I had verified that there were no obvious food blobs stuck to his shirt, but I had not thought to make sure he had a belt on his pants. I tried to keep track of the whereabouts of his belts because he is utterly unaware of his appearance or placement of clothing. He has been known to set the standard for "plumber's crack" reveals. We went to services, which were packed with other families all looking very tidy. All of my children were behaving brilliantly during the sermon. I began to feel pride, that kind of pride that makes you feel hope that everyone else is noticing how tidy, well behaved and nice my family was acting.

Then came the portion of the service in which individuals were asked to come forward to pray by a large wooden cross laid in front of the congregation on a set of risers in front of the altar. As soon as the pastor made the announcement for people to come forward to pray, my oldest son jumped up and placed himself at the foot of the cross in a kneeling position that resembled child's pose in yoga. I ran after him and placed myself in front of him farther up the steps. Once I finished praying, I turned around and noticed two preteen boys in the front pew giggling hysterically and pointing at my son. I also noticed several adults around them suppressing grins. This was the opposite of the mood of the moment in which we were supposed to be contemplating our humility, so I looked over at my son. I discovered that not only had he forgotten to put a belt on, but he had evidently put on his brother's very small underwear that morning instead of his own. That means that when he knelt down, his underwear that did not fit up past his hips, slid way down and his waistband similarly slid down past his buttocks. My son was oblivious to the fact that he was mooning the entire congregation and giving full proof of his male sex, all the while vigorously praying while kneeling at the cross! Furthermore, I knew that if I brought this to his attention, he would immediately think it hilarious and would start loud laughing and become less coordinated and therefore less likely to be able to hitch up his pants. I realized that I had only two choices, to laugh at the absurdity of the situation and my own foolish pride that thought I could escape the humanity of my family, or try to make an unfixable situation worse. I made the only good choice available. I laughed. I laughed at my own hubris that I thought I could pull off perfection and I laughed at the thought of so many worshippers getting an eyeful of my son's anatomy when they were least expecting it.

Isn't it always this way for our children and families? Just when we think we are getting to the place of just right, something absurd occurs and we are faced with the choice of being inflexible and getting stuck on what we wanted or learning to roll with the situation and enjoy the absurdity. If there is anything my children have taught me, it is to laugh and see how absurd and foolish my notions of family quality are in comparison to the pleasure of enjoying what comes my way.

You also have to be willing to see the absurdity in treatment and mental health providers, not just in yourself and your kids. Many parents I see get stuck in the idea that if they were to have the best therapist or do treatment the very best way, then their child or teen would be more likely to get better. This is simply not true. Speaking as a mental health professional, I and my ilk are not perfect. We have plenty of moments of absurdity during treatment. The magic ingredient for good treatment outcome is not a perfect therapist. The magic happens when you, your therapist and your child work together to learn how to manage and overcome anxiety regardless of the circumstances. Exposure does not have to be perfectly graduated because life does not present perfectly graduated doses of exposure. The therapist's wording does not have to be perfect and your child does not always have to like your therapist. You just have to all be on the same page about learning to face and manage anxiety while simultaneously doing all the things that kids are supposed to do. I have had parents want to quit treatment because their child hated a particular exposure and became uncharacteristically (up until that point) oppositional because they believed that this meant that I had not done a good job of making each exposure step similarly easy. I have had parents get offended because I mentioned the child's diagnosis when they did not want their child to hear that they had a diagnosis. (This is a practice I disagree with but try to respect when the parents are adamant. Children deserve to know that they are not alone and that many people have worked hard to develop treatment especially for them.) Parents have wanted to stop treatment because their child hated coming to treatment, or because the treats and prizes I had in my office were not to their child's liking. The point is that all of these examples are failures in perceiving absurdity and failures at having good humor.

Let me illustrate one example of what happens when the parent is able to find the funny in the moment and how it helps the child or teen. I was working with a girl who was a competitive ice skater who'd had a recent bad fall in a competition and became afraid of jumping while practicing or competing. This is a big problem because figure skaters fall a lot, whether they are practicing or competing. She and I began practice by doing exposure to making mistakes while jumping up in the air while on land. We stood in my office, jumped up high in the air, and twirled around and then fell gracelessly. Once she got comfortable with this, we advanced to jumping high and twirling while using the hand and leg motions that one might use for a real jump. She was having some good success jumping higher and risking a fall. I was encouraging her to really go for it. I am not an ice skater, so I admit I was pretty clunky compared to her graceful attempts, but I went at it with enthusiasm. I demonstrated what I thought was a mighty leap and as I came down and kicked out my leg, my rubber shoe sole caught the hem of my elastic waisted skirt. The net result was that I completely pulled down my skirt as I landed in my imitation of a graceful hands out in the air and standing tall landing. I was standing there in my stockings and slip (thank God!) in this absurd pose with my patient looking at me with a shocked expression. I began laughing. Then the patient's mother began laughing, and finally the patient began laughing. We laughed so much that we could not end the session without bursting into laughter. I then told the patient that she had thought that falling was the worst thing that could happen, when really it was losing your skirt that was the worst thing. She was able to use that silly image of me, skirt-less and trying to land in a not so graceful rendition of her landing, as a motivator to stop taking her fear of falling so seriously. She rapidly made progress with her treatment and skating lessons on the ice. Her mother told me afterwards that she entertained her skating team with the story of my skirt-less landing and would giggle about this before going into competition to reduce her nerves about performance.

> **HOT TIP**
>
> Nothing about recovery is so serious that you cannot find something absurd about the situation. Learn to enjoy the absurdity of your child or teen having to face fears when their body and mind simultaneously want to avoid them, even though they want to get better.

Finding the funny in exposure

Laughter is a frequent sound in my clinic when we are at work. My staff and I enjoy helping our patients get through exposure practice because we appreciate how absurd the situations are that exposure practice necessitates. Here are some examples to help you get your creative good humor mindset in gear.

- Trying to get a screaming preteen to eat a frosted donut when their contamination fears have convinced them that the donut has been contaminated by the clerk's hands and saliva. Assigning this same kid to have to eat a donut every day.

- Doing social anxiety exposure by walking through the shopping mall wearing a hot pink feather boa with a boy who is also wearing a hot pink feather boa and trying to get people to notice us and make critical stares or comments and not being able to get anyone to appear to notice us.

- Having a family use the goodbye statement, "Goodbye and I hope you die!" to help their preschooler practice overcoming fears of separation and then realizing that the preschool teacher and other parents overheard their exposure practice.

- Having an eleven-year-old child practice using the elevator by themselves to develop independence and then having the elevator randomly stop and get stuck. The parent gets teary-eyed about how terrified and traumatized her child must be. When the repairman finally fixed the elevator, we discovered the child was singing "99 bottles of beer on the wall" while waiting. As soon as he saw us he announced, "Getting stuck wasn't as bad as I thought it would be. I could tell that you were trying to rescue me. My friends will think this is so cool!"

- Giving a home assignment of hugging and kissing the family dog to help a boy get over his fear of feces. Hearing that this boy then would go and kiss his parents on the mouth without telling them that he just kissed the dog. Also playing catch in the backyard with little plastic baggies of frozen dog feces.

- A parent successfully ignored a screaming preteen boy who was being treated for severe oppositional behavior. The parent was in a busy parking lot while her son had a severe tantrum and she stepped outside the car and locked the door while turning her back to him and ignoring him. The boy started screaming that he was being abused and several bystanders ended up calling the police. When the policeman arrived, he discovered that the boy was just trying to get out of a necessary timeout and whispered to the parent that they were doing a good job.

Do you see why my job can be so much fun? And why your child's recovery can be so much fun? Each of these situations I described is similar to every child's and teen's potential reaction during treatment. We have to do things that seem absurd, given your child's anxiety or the cultural norms for behavior. Exposure gives your child or teen the opportunity to hone their sense of good humor because it really is funny that they have to practice the sort of things that other kids might do easily or that others might think seems odd. Trying to drag a socially anxious kid to a playground or a party so they can learn to have fun most definitely has a degree of absurdity, especially when you realize that being able to go play or to attend a party is every kid's dream.

EXERCISES TO IMPROVE GOOD HUMOR IN GENERAL

1. Start asking your child several times a week, "What was the funniest thing that happened today?" Don't let them evade the question by saying "Nothing." Ask them to dig and find the funniest thing out of an otherwise dull day.

2. Start sharing the funniest thing that happened during your day at the family dinner, bedtime or other times when you are together.

3. Have a competition to find the funniest video or meme. Declare a theme, such as hamsters, cats, ponies or dogs. Everyone shares their selection of the funniest video. The winner gets to pick dessert.

4. Make it a habit to watch comedy together, whether it is movies or funny shows on television. Be careful to avoid shows that feature lots of sarcasm. Teach your family that we are the family who laughs together and finds fun together.

5. Download a free laugh track app and play this when you need it to elevate your sense of humor, such as before picking kids up from school, or when about to enforce the rule to do homework or exposure practice.

6. Have your child or teen read comedy. There are many funny books for children and teens that you can find

by searching for the term "comedy" paired with other topics, for example, romantic teen comedy, children's comedy, etc.

7. Be willing to laugh when funny things happen during exposure practice. It gives your child or teen a cue to perceive absurdity.

8. Share your own stories of absurdity in which you were the featured fool and had a good laugh about yourself. This provides a healthy role model. My children have never asked me about my successes, but they have often asked about my failures and my most embarrassing moments.

9. Ask your child or teen to tell you what the most fun thing is about their treatment, or their exposure practice. This encourages them to shift perspective and to learn to search for the fun in the middle of the struggle.

10. Be willing to laugh about yourself in front of your child. Show them that you do not take yourself too seriously so they can learn how to do it too.

11. Ask your child to tell you what has been the funniest thing about the exposure practices they have done. You will be surprised, because often they can tell you some pretty funny things.

CHAPTER 7

Uncertainty and Risk Taking Are a Parent's Best Friend

Intolerance of uncertainty is a component of anxiety that is worth special mention. It is a mindset that makes people especially prone to worry. When you, or your child, has intolerance of uncertainty, it means that you find it difficult to feel comfortable and calm when you do not know the outcome. If you are intolerant of uncertainty, you likely try to eliminate uncertainty by focusing upon the worst-case scenario and take the "better safe than sorry" approach to life.

If you, or your child, worries, then you try to eliminate the perception of uncertainty by narrowing your focus to all the things that might possibly go wrong. Your intolerance of uncertainty makes you prefer to get a guarantee that things will go well and you might often get caught up in seeking reassurance that things go well instead of just calmly waiting to see what happens. Surprises might even become something that you, or your child, dislike because it means not knowing what will happen. For example, I have many patients who suffer from worry who tell me that they would rather know what their birthday gifts are ahead of time instead of having to wait and be surprised. I also have teens tell me that they would rather get bad news about a test or college entrance application than have to wait longer for good news. The problem with focusing upon the worst-case scenario is that it triggers the false alarm of anxiety because the brain cannot tell the difference between an imagined and a real worst-case scenario. Additionally, if you are prone to worry, then your automatic fear alarm that gets triggered makes you think worry must be important because you are feeling so scared. Whew!

Reassurance seeking

One of the most obvious signs of intolerance of uncertainty is reassurance seeking. Reassurance seeking is what happens when you, or your child, try to get information that stacks the odds in favor of a good outcome. It can consist of trying to get someone's opinion or researching on the Internet to get information that makes you feel reassured. Reassurance seeking seems like a good idea and feels like being responsible, but it can amount to a way to make anxiety worse by asking the same question over and over, often in slightly different ways. It can sound like this, "Do you think that the other kids will be nice to me? Do you think any of the boys will be mean? Do you think the teacher will make the other kids be nice? Do you think the headmistress will punish the mean kids?" It could also sound like this, "Do you think I am as good looking as other kids? Do you think that someone will ask me out? Do you think I will get married someday? What would happen if no one wants to go out with me?" Another version might look like this, "Are you sure I don't have cancer? How do you know

I won't die from cancer? What do you think will make me die someday? Do you think it will be cancer? What if the doctors cannot detect cancer if I have it?" If your kid seeks reassurance you will know it because they keep circling around the same issue and nothing you say is enough to satisfy their anxiety. If they are really intolerant of uncertainty, then they might even get more anxious when you say something that they misinterpret as being the "wrong" or "bad" answer. For example, you answer a reassurance seeking question about getting sick like this, "Those bumps are probably just bug bites and not cancer." Then your child looks more alarmed and says, "So you think there might be a chance I have cancer! You said probably!"

You might accidentally get caught up with reassurance seeking too. I encounter this when parents ask me every single time we meet whether or not their child or teen is making progress, or whether or not their child will make a full recovery. I see reassurance seeking when parents repeatedly ask their child if they are feeling less anxious. I see it when parents repeatedly ask about my credentials, background and the exact number of similar patients I have treated. I see it when parents repeatedly text their children to see if they are safe, healthy, having fun or doing well, or when parents repeatedly check the GPS locator for their child's whereabouts to make sure their child is in a safe location. If you are one of these parents, then you are accidentally being a negative role model of intolerance of uncertainty and using worry and reassurance seeking as a way to handle risk. Reassurance seeking is a form of negative reinforcement that always backfires and makes anxiety worse. When you are an example of reassurance seeking and risk avoidance then you discourage your child from taking necessary risks and learning to tolerate the uncertainty of life.

> ## HOT TIP
> Giving in to reassurance seeking undermines your child's ability to trust their own opinion and helps them become addicted to needing the opinion of an authority, such as a parent.

Reassurance seeking has a negative effect on self-confidence. When you, or your child, engage in reassurance seeking, you undermine your ability to trust your own opinion. Each time you seek verification that something is safe, you then erode your ability to trust the non-anxious reasonable part of your mind and you become less able to manage doubt. Repeatedly giving in to doubt by seeking an outside opinion cripples your child from being able to take risks in decision making. It accidentally teaches them that only a special authority is capable of making a decision and determine which risks to take. When your child gets caught in this trap, they are robbed of their ability to develop mastery and a sense of competence at managing life.

My youngest son is a good example of what happens when fear of risk taking and making mistakes gets in the way of normal development. He was born with the tendency to want to get things right and to avoid mistakes or frustration. He was ready to walk for at least three months before he took his first step. He would cruise around all the furniture and could not be tempted to take a single step no matter what we did. When he did take his first steps, he walked carefully and beautifully across the room and then promptly sat down before he evidenced even a wobble. He then refrained from walking for the next two weeks until he did it again and walked everywhere without falling because he was clearly being very careful. This was the way my son did everything, with too much thinking about it ahead of time and then a very cautious entry and quick exit before things went badly. This is in stark contrast to his brother, who fell all the time and would repeatedly attempt walking and running despite not being able to go more than three steps without falling or crashing into the furniture or walls. His older brother had the benefit of living with a disability that made doing anything that required the use of his muscles clumsy and clunky. He just got used to it and learned that the only truly useful thing was to keep trying until he got what he wanted, even if it cost him bruises or people staring at him.

Later, when my younger son was nine years old, our family went downhill skiing. My oldest son with cerebral palsy loved downhill skiing, despite his frequent falls or swerving off the trail only to fill his nostrils and mouth with snow due to a faceplant. My youngest son, on the other hand, roared with disapproval and worry about every potential fall or mistake. He put on his skiing gear and protested incessantly about not knowing how to ski. On his first downhill run, he fell after about ten meters of skiing, had a huge tantrum and then refused to ski. It took ignoring his tantrum and insisting he get comfortable with falling and then leaving him behind, knowing that he would not want to be left alone, before he made several cautious downhill runs and announced that he liked skiing. His brother's devil may care attitude was in sharp contrast on this same trip to the resort. He went on the ski lift alone to the highest run and came to the bottom covered in snow from face to skis. He proudly announced that his run was a success because he stayed on the trail, did not get a bloody nose from snow being forced up his nostrils due to a fall and made it to the bottom.

Now that my youngest son is a young adult who has undergone a lot of therapy, he admits that he regrets all the times he refused to try new things because he feared not doing well, being embarrassed or feeling shy. He is making up for lost time by deliberately pushing himself to do things that scare him because, "Mom, I do not want to live like that. It's no fun and it just made me sad. I would rather be scared and do the things I really like!" His older brother, on the other hand, likes to recall the time we went downhill skiing and I witnessed him accidentally veer off the trail onto a four-and-a-half-meter drop into deep snow. I was worried that he had injured himself when I peeked over the steep drop. He announced to me, "Mom, did you see that? I almost stuck the landing on that jump!" That is the difference between the one who always tries to get reassurance and avoid risks and the one who embraces the risk in the hopes of doing something big.

Embracing risk

What do non-anxious kids and parents do that works so well with managing uncertainty? They embrace risk because they realize that risk taking is beneficial. Research on those who are rapid learners shows they take more risks and make more mistakes early in the process of learning than perfectionistic students (Kim, 2016; SINTEF, 2015; Vorobyev *et al.*, 2016). Instead of wasting time trying to get it right, they just start trying until they get better and eventually get it right. Non-anxious children and adults say things like "There is no point in worrying. I might as well enjoy things while they are good."

They realize that the content of worry is imaginary and is therefore not worth thinking about. They also say things like "You only live once" and "Better to die trying than to never have tried at all." They acknowledge that bad things could happen but let go of the need to take special measures to prevent bad outcomes because they accept that there is no guaranteed way to prevent risk or random tragedy. They prefer to live in the moment and to take enjoyment whenever it occurs, knowing that someday a painful event might indeed occur. They do not want to waste time spending their mental head space on worry.

By contrast, those who worry have worry-supporting beliefs that make it difficult to embrace uncertainty. Worriers believe that their worry has a protective factor. Have you ever thought, or said aloud, "It's a parent's job to worry" or "Someone has to be the responsible one and make sure all the bases are covered" or "Someone has to make sure they get home safely?" When you, or your child, believe that your worry helps you manage the uncertainty and risk of living, then you set up yourself, and your child, for failure at overcoming anxiety. Worry confers the false illusion of control that prevents you from learning to embrace risk as part of the adventure of living. Your child needs to learn that risk taking brings delight in newfound skills and positive changes in self-confidence. Part of the fun of doing exposure practice is creating a sense of adventure and exploration about what will happen when we try scary things. 1 try to help families replace fear of uncertainty with curiosity and open-mindedness about all the possibilities that might occur.

Additionally, overparenting or being overprotective can prevent your child from being able to develop leadership, a skill necessary for becoming a successful parent or employee

(Zhengguang *et al.*, 2019). Leadership is defined by the ability to see what is needed in the situation and to be able to assess the resources needed to help the group succeed and to engage in self-sacrificing behaviors without having to wait for the approval or blessing of others. When you step in too often to help your child when they feel distress, you become the expert at being the leader without mentoring the same skills in your child.

> ### PARENT RESILIENCY RULE 12
> Reframe your child's life with anxiety and uncertainty about their future, as an adventure to be explored with curiosity and enthusiasm.

Frequently, kids and parents want me to guarantee that nothing bad will happen when we do exposure practice. This is impossible. Contamination exposure might increase risk for illness. Social exposure might result in embarrassment. Sometimes a truly terrible random thing might happen to a child's family. What I want your child to learn is that they no longer have to worry about these things and that, even if the worst-case scenario occurs, they can trust themselves to survive and thrive. I want you and your child to become aware of the amazing ability of human beings to literally overcome anything. If you think about it, one of the truly remarkable things about human beings is that we have im- mense capacity to survive the very worst events and have done so for millennia. So I would rather have you and your child approach recovery as an adventure in risk taking than viewing treatment as a guaranteed way to feel good.

HOT TIP

View your child's recovery as an adventure in risk taking that, like all adventures, involves facing risk, peril and great challenges that ultimately lead to the central character's greatness.

Recovery should be an adventure

When you treat recovery as an adventure, you help your child get unstuck from having to feel good and having to feel safe. You help your child refocus upon daring to do things that lead to long-term joy and mastery. You help them enlarge their vision and learn that good things come to those who take risks and face fear. One of the problems with being intolerant of uncertainty is that your child's thinking becomes narrow and inflexible. Their mind quickly gravitates to the most negative thoughts and overlooks the neutral and positive options that are also present. For example, if your child is fearful of vomiting and scans others for signs of illness and avoids school whenever they hear that another child has a stomach upset, they are not able to imagine other thoughts when they hear mention of vomit. They are unable to imagine that they are not ill, to imagine that others do not always have a vomit-inducing illness or to imagine that kids vomiting in school is pretty rare. They cannot imagine all the fun they can have talking to friends or learning what the teacher is presenting. They also cannot imagine giving up scanning for signs of imminent gastrointestinal illness in others. They will be stuck desperately looking for reassurance. They need to practice exposure to uncertainty and risk taking that challenges all of their fears.

Let me illustrate. One family I was working with had a son who worried about every decision, every new activity and every time his parents left him at home. He would barrage his parents with questions about what the best thing was to do, which video game to play, which friend to invite over, which subject to study first or which sport to join at school. He wanted to make sure that he did not waste his time with being unproductive or by doing things that would not give him the maximal pleasure. He got caught up in evaluating everything he did. He also worried about safety. He researched traffic safety, safety records for the type of cars his parents drove, safety of the sports he might join or the best ways to be nutritious or healthy. His parents initially viewed their son as being more mature and responsible than his peers until he began grilling them about their driving habits, drinking habits and refrained from making a final choice for sports or clubs to join at school. He would text them while they were out to remind them to avoid drinking and driving and to eat healthy foods.

When he came into treatment, he justified his behaviors as being an extension of his love for his parents and his desire to live a good life and accumulate a resume that would guarantee him an entrance into a top-notch college. When asked about general intolerance of uncertainty, he and his parents laughed and said that the patient was the world's best planner and was always prepared for everything. They pointed out with pride that he always had a first aid kit in his backpack and several back up plans when they went on vacations in case anything went wrong. They also pointed out that he liked a printed itinerary for every vacation and had kept elaborate planners since age ten for all of his activities. He would get upset if he could not fill out his planners, had trouble sleeping due to worry and not feeling adequately prepared and reported that his friends would get annoyed with him about his planning and preparation for even the simplest of activities. He also disliked any surprises and wanted to always know the plan for any situation. He also mentioned that he had lost friends who always waited until they got together to finalize plans because he found this so upsetting. He had clearly lost his flexibility and ability to adapt to his adolescent peers.

For treatment, we did lots of exposure practice that consisted of setting up surprising and unknown situations that he had to embrace by going into them unprepared. Unprepared meant without taking supplies for potential emergencies, thirst, hunger, changes in weather or changes in location. This kid had taken the Scout's motto to "Be prepared" too seriously. It also meant only using his planner for writing down things he might actually forget or for reminders of due dates for assignments or exams. He was not allowed to ask peers for the plans ahead of time when there was no plan. We also had his parents change their language by saying, "Looks like it will be an adventure. Let's see what fun can be had." We had his parents stop giving him itineraries for vacations and outings and created mystery adventures in which the parents selected a new place to go without giving any hints. The patient had to report back on five discoveries and three positives about their mystery adventure. I also had the patient read some biographies about famous explorers and then report back on what he learned about the benefits of that person being willing to embrace risk taking and adventure. We also talked about his recovery in terms of it being an adventure in risk taking and discovering the advantages of unpreparedness. Additionally, I had several solo sessions with the parents to talk about changing their perspective on the value of embracing risk and viewing their son's life as an adventure both for themselves and their son. I explained that a willingness to take risks could add zest to their lives as opposed to only doing things that are predictable and safe. This brings us to my last point about embracing uncertainty.

Zesty living versus safe living

There is another disadvantage to always living in a manner that feels safe, predictable and low in risk. It is boredom. Living a life that is predictable and always goes a certain way ends up creating a prison of boredom. Human beings need novelty, challenges and the unexpected to grow and flourish throughout our lifespan. When you let your child or teen repeatedly avoid challenges that provoke anxiety, you accidentally help them narrow down the scope of their life along with their dreams for the future. When you let your child always play it safe, you prevent them from discovering that they can step into the unknown and discover that marvelous things can occur when they do things that are not in the guaranteed comfort zone.

Research on mental and physical wellness shows us that the people who have the best quality of life and the best brain health are those who repeatedly put themselves in situations that are challenging and demand the acquisition of new skills. Elders who take classes and learn new languages and new hobbies can prevent disease and dementia (Leanos *et al.*, 2019). International youth and young adult programs, such as Outward Bound and National Outdoor Leadership Workshop, place teens and young adults in difficult and dangerous wilderness settings for the purpose of helping participants learn that they have more ability to handle and overcome challenges than they previously realized. Youth who complete these programs frequently report feeling exhilarated and more capable and often perform more successfully in their daily activities than prior to the program. Many young adults credit military boot camp and military life with giving them important skills in accepting, handling and overcoming challenges. If you did something unexpected and challenging, such as backpacking through a foreign country, a semester abroad in a foreign country or finishing a marathon, you know what I am talking about. You probably use this experience as an important reference point in which you expanded your vision of who you were and what you could accomplish. You probably realize that many people enjoy taking on big challenges, such as training to complete a long and difficult race or buying a fixer upper to remodel even though they have no background in sports or home repair. It is also likely the reason so many people took up new hobbies during the global COVID-19 pandemic. They were seeking to avoid boredom by taking on new challenges. They were doing the opposite of avoiding uncertainty and stepping into the challenge of risk taking and embracing the unknown.

HOT TIP

Living a safe, predictable life that never takes risks kills adventure, takes the zest out of life and guarantees boredom. Why would you want to do that to your child?

Zesty living means inviting excitement into your life, which means allowing and creating the danger that occurs from taking risks. This happens every single time your child practices exposure. They learn to step toward the possibility of recovery, even though they are deliberately inviting risk and potential danger. For example, I recently worked with a family whose seven-year-old feared a kidnapper or terrorist would invade her bedroom at night. The parents also feared that a predator might kidnap their child when the child was out of sight of an adult and they emphasized being cautious when in public and staying within view of a parent or teacher at all times. They sought treatment because their daughter would not play alone, would not sleep alone nor sleep without the lights on. This meant that she and her parents were sleep deprived. She had elaborate checking and reassurance seeking rituals for making sure all the doors and windows were locked at night and would not allow herself to be left alone at a friend's house to play.

For her exposure practice, I had her place signs outside her bedroom and outside her window that gave directions for any would-be kidnappers or terrorists: "Little girl in this room." We unlocked her bedroom windows and left the front and back door unlocked when she was in the house and at nighttime during sleep until she overcame her fear. We read stories about true kidnappings of children and wrote stories about what would happen were she to be kidnapped. We also had her parents tell her goodnight and mention that this goodnight was her final one because she would be kidnapped or murdered that night by an intruder. We did all of this without providing reassurance or reminding her that "this was just exposure." Additionally, we had her walk around the block by herself, ride her bike alone around the neighborhood and do similar things that previously felt dangerous to her and her parents.

Once she overcame her anxiety about being alone and out of sight of her parents, we had her bike to her friend's houses by herself and leave her parents at restaurants to go to the toilet by herself. We had her go to the playground by herself to play with other kids. She ended up becoming very independent and, without any coaching on my part, made some new neighborhood friends because she was able to travel outside her house alone. She also discovered that the world outside of her house was a fun and safe place which was in contradiction to her fear and her parents' fear about child kidnapping and pedophiles. Her parents discovered that their child was much more outgoing than they had realized and that she easily made friends and loved playing outdoors. They also discovered that it was really nice to sleep alone and to have time alone while their daughter was playing outside the house. They also admitted that prior to therapy they falsely believed that the rates for interpersonal crime were at an all-time high. They did not really believe the research that shows that the interpersonal crime rates in the United States have dramatically declined in the past forty years and only agreed to do exposure therapy because they were desperate to get some uninterrupted sleep. They learned that exposure practice helped them change their beliefs about danger and accept that they, too, had been affected by worry, reassurance seeking and intolerance of worry.

The exposure practice that this family did might seem extreme or counterintuitive, because shouldn't a parent protect their young child from the darker parts of life? Shouldn't good parents try to shield their young children from information about kidnapping, burglaries and other things that might alarm them? Ideally, we would be able to have all children avoid unnecessary awareness of the base side of humanity until they are developmentally ready. The problem is that anxiety takes away this option because it pushes your child to imagine the worst without anyone having to tell them ahead of time. Anxiety also forces your child's imagination to think of the scariest things that we all fear and find distasteful, even when no one has given them this information ahead of time. So, you have two choices. Do exposure to all the things that your child's anxious imagination has already imagined and take a pre-emptive strike at all the directions their anxious imagination will go if left untreated. Your only other choice is to erase your child's imagination from their mind. You need to be willing to make an exception for your child's anxiety when their anxiety gets focused upon things that you normally would not discuss such as sexual topics, violence, crime or breaking the rules. You need to be bold in showing your child with exposure practice that what we imagine is never something real and never something to worry about.

So, I want you to think of risk taking as a means to creating zesty living for yourself and for your child. Playing it safe guarantees a boring life with few opportunities for the joy of discovery. It is sad indeed to talk to adults who recount how their fear made them avoid important opportunities, such as going to college, trying out for a spot on a team, volunteering for a new position, asking someone out, making new friends or trying to cultivate the career of their dreams. These adults all realized in hindsight that they wished they could have understood that the risk of failing, making a mistake, getting really anxious or of feeling humiliation was worth the attempt to explore, create and expand their world. The only way your child can learn that risk taking is part of living an adventurous life is through repeated practice. Exposure is one way to create this practice opportunity that leads to zesty living. This is most certainly a reason to feel good humored. The anxiety disorder that seems to be an obstacle is also the opportunity to mix things up and make life more fun and adventuresome because full recovery necessitates it!

Part of successful living means being willing to charge into uncertain situations with the attitude that something good might happen instead of the anxious child's motto of "What if something bad happens?" Children and adults who overcome anxiety learn to think that uncertainty offers an opportunity for new and exciting things to happen, things that could lead to a richer life. They try out for the school play, sports team or student leadership group because they see that the only way to increase the likelihood of good change is to increase risk by daring to fail in the pursuit of gaining a new opportunity. You need to understand that your child needs to learn to face and enter uncertain situations without reassurance *and with the full acknowledgment that something might go wrong.* When I conduct exposure practice with my patients, I avoid telling them that everything is perfectly safe and harmless. If a child asks me, "Will I get sick if I touch these things and stop washing my hands?" I make sure to answer them, "I don't know, but even if you get sick, there is something much worse that will happen if you avoid touching this. Your anxiety will run your life instead of you. Now let's go ahead and touch it." If a worried child tells me, "I can't go and ask that boy to play with me. What if he says no or makes fun of me?" I reply with, "I don't know what he will say, but you have no chance of playing with him if you do not ask him. If you don't ask him, you will also have a 100 percent chance of always feeling shy and anxious and accidentally convincing other kids that you do not want to play with them because you never ask them." You tell your child the truth about the possibility of something unpleasant happening while emphasizing the benefit of taking the risk just the same. Children and adults always regret opportunities not taken and almost never regret the risks they took in service of gaining an important goal.

EXERCISES TO HELP YOUR CHILD EMBRACE UNCERTAINTY AND RISK TAKING

1. Put a ban on giving reassurance and encourage your child to make up their own mind. You can point out that they are reassurance seeking and highlight the uncertainty, for example, "Looks like you are trying to get reassurance for your anxiety. I cannot say anything one way or the other." If you are uncomfortable just saying this, you can blame it on the child's therapist or doctors: "Doctor's orders are that I not give you any reassurance. I cannot say anything one way or another." Then give your child a reward and some praise for not pestering you for more reassurance.

2. Turn the tables on your child and ask them "What do you think?" and then do not answer or confirm their reassurance seeking, for example, "Well, what do you think about this? What do you think you should do?"

3. Talk about times where you took a big risk and why you took the risk. Don't just talk about the times your risk taking paid off, such as trying out for a part in the play and getting a part. Also share about the times that it did not go well, but how you felt proud of yourself for at least trying out. Help your child understand that regret is the consequence of action not taken and zesty living comes only from taking risks.

4. Start using language that indicates that nothing is certain in life, but that this is OK because it makes life

an adventure. Explain the idea of an adventure, or an epic journey, in which the main character enters into a known risky and dangerous journey whose completion will guarantee something important and valuable along with great personal growth. Reading stories together that allow you talk about the heroic journey, such as J.K. Rowling's Harry Potter stories or the *The Lion, the Witch and the Wardrobe* by C.S. Lewis, will give you opportunities to talk about the adventure of living a life inherent with substantial risks and the potential for great gains should one willingly enter into those risks. Be sure to talk about what happens to the characters who avoid risk and who cheat in order to avoid the hard work necessary to achieve something great.

5. Watch movies together that portray the epic journey of a someone building great character. Ask your child about what made the main character so heroic and ask how they handled the unknown and the dangers that were confronted. Make the parallel with overcoming anxiety and ask your child how they could be more like the heroic main character in their journey against anxiety.

6. Ask your child or teen to identify the most heroic thing they could do to battle their anxiety. Encourage them to do this heroic thing and to live into their potential as a strong and capable human being. Reframe going to therapy as being a way to become heroic in their own life struggle against fear. Start believing this yourself.

7. If your child is young enough to believe in a superhero,

ask them to pretend to be their favorite superhero when confronting their anxiety and doing exposure practice. Let them dress up as their favorite superhero while doing exposure practice. I find that when I do this with young children they often acquire the bravery of the superhero when wearing a costume and then can transfer this superpower to the rest of their day.

CHAPTER 8

Gratitude Is My
New Attitude

The idea of gratitude has become pretty trendy in the twenty-first century. You may have seen all the trendy signs, mugs and journals that remind people to be thankful. You might even have one of those cute diaries made specifically for writing down things for which you are grateful. You might also be the sort of person whose place of worship has specific prayers of gratitude that you say during worship. There is a good chance that you consider gratitude to be a good idea but one that sounds a bit trite and hackneyed due to advertising and social media posts. What you might not realize is the immense potential of gratitude to improve mental wellness and cultivate optimism and grit.

What is gratitude?

When researchers study gratitude, they are referring to a specific state of mind in which a person believes in the goodness of life, even when they are aware of suffering or experiencing suffering (Emmons and McCullough, 2003). It is the ability to figure out where good comes from and to acknowledge that the source is outside of ourselves. It is the realization that all of life is a gift. It is much more than a momentary feeling of pleasure about something that you like or prefer. It is a recognition that something wonderful has happened no matter how small or unnoticed by others. So you can see that gratitude is more than making a list and counting the number of good things that have happened or saying "Thank you."

Gratitude is also the psychological opposite of entitlement. People who feel gratitude are also feeling humility and are aware that they do not deserve the things for which they are grateful. They avoid taking good events and happy moments for granted and are well aware that if the good things in their life were taken away they would miss them. They also realize that the good things in their life are gifts and never entitlements. Grateful people born into privileged circumstances realize they did nothing special to deserve the blessings of their privilege. Grateful children and adults are able to contrast their moments of gratitude with past moments of deprivation or empathy for those who are deprived of the thing for which they are grateful. For example, when a family had their house burn down on Christmas Eve, I heard several of my son's friends talking about this unfortunate family and telling each other "I am so lucky I get to have Christmas and have a house. It would be awful to lose your house and all of your Christmas presents. We should do something." I have also heard my youngest son tell the parents in his kid and parent therapy group, "Parents, I am telling you this. Your kid needs you to take away their phone if you want them to stop being so rude and refusing to cooperate. I used to hate it when my mom did this, but it worked really well. I love having my phone and I hated my mom for taking it away and insisting that I be nicer and do chores. I am so glad that she did that. Your kid won't know how lucky they are to have their phone unless you take it away!" This statement was especially meaningful because my son had never said anything that hinted at gratitude for my parenting and had a long tradition of reminding me of how annoying and mean I was as a parent. His statement demonstrated that he no longer took his phone, nor his mother's efforts at raising him, for granted, at least in that moment.

Benefits of gratitude

There have been more than fifteen thousand studies conducted on the benefits of gratitude and gratitude is now considered to be the mother skill of mental wellness (Tala, 2019). When a child learns to be grateful, they create the foundation for the other character skills that lead to resilience and grit. Here is a partial list of the known benefits of helping yourself and your child cultivate a grateful perspective on life, including your child's anxiety disorder. People who have a grateful mindset are happier in life and in their close relationships, more optimistic, more resilient after experiencing a trauma, more charitable with time and money, make better grades, earn more money and live an average of seven years longer than those who are not. They also experience fewer illnesses, are ten times less likely to smoke, less likely to get into fights and experience less envy, materialism and possessiveness in relationships (American Psychological Association, 2020; Randolph, 2017). Lastly, they have lower blood pressure, less cardiovascular disease and lower levels of anxiety and depression than those who are not skilled in gratitude (Yoshimura & Berzins, 2017). This list of benefits is so powerful that it inspired me to begin writing down my moments of gratitude fourteen years ago. I continue this habit today because it has been so beneficial.

Gratitude also motivates us to help others. One study had one group keep track of hassles and compared that group of people to others who were instructed to keep track of things they were grateful for. Over the ten weeks of the study the group differences were profound. The ones who tracked gratitude ended up sleeping better, exercising more, feeling happier, spontaneously helping others and spontaneously feeling and acting with more kindness. The gratitude trackers also reported improved relationships with family and friends (Algoe, Gable & Maisel, 2010; Williams & Bartlett, 2014). This is powerful stuff, especially when you consider that one of the more common complaints I hear from parents, supervisors and educators is that children, teens and young adults are annoyingly entitled. Entitlement is the moral and attitudinal opposite of gratitude. It is the belief that good things are a birthright and deprivation from privilege is unjust. If your child has you worried because of their sense of entitlement, then you need to pay close attention to what can be done to cultivate gratitude. Their future mental health and morality depends upon it.

Another challenge to gratitude is the *self-serving bias*, which is a close relative of the previously mentioned attribution bias. The self-serving bias states that people tend to take all the credit for the good and blame others for the bad. For example, a child on a winning team who made a goal or assisted a goal will tend to think that they were instrumental to the team's victory and, conversely, if their team loses, they will find themselves blameless and quickly point out the failure of their teammates as the reason for the team's loss. It's the same reason your boss will take all the credit for the team's hard work and forget that they would be nowhere without all the work of the team, and then sharply criticizes everyone's work the next week. The self-serving bias is the opposite of taking personal responsibility when things go wrong and the opposite of being grateful for all of the good that is present.

One way that I see parents interfering with the growth of gratitude and accidentally enhancing the self-serving bias in their kids is demonstrated in how they handle their child's participation in a group project that includes less skilled children, or children who refuse to do their fair share of the group's work. Many of the parents I see get anxious and angry about the possibility of their child getting a lower grade. They tell their child that this situation is unfair, that their child's work is much better and more valuable to the group. They might even try to persuade the teacher to give their child a better grade than the other children in the group or try to have their child switched to a seemingly better group. They put down the work of the other children and accidentally encourage blaming others for a bad outcome. They might even blame the teacher if the group grade is less than stellar. If you have done this, what do you think you are teaching to your child? You are accidentally teaching them that they are entitled to a good grade every time they do their work, that they should never have to share responsibility and that it is a terrible thing to have to work with people who are less than perfect. It also teaches your child to point the finger at someone else when they are unhappy instead of learning how to successfully adapt to the situation or cooperate so that they inspire others to do better.

Here is what I wish every parent could do when faced with their child's mistake or failure. Turn the situation into a growth experience by doing the following. Tell your child something like this, "No one gets to have a perfect team in which everyone is the best player, best student or best at everything. Part of being in a group or on a team is learning how to work together when you are not the same in skill level or interest level. Everyone on the team always has something to contribute. Since you can do some of this well, then you can help the team with the part that you do well. Your job is to help the others with what you do well and to help them be a part of the team too." The parents would then refuse to intervene with the teacher and instead tell their child to talk to the teacher about how to get the other kids more involved. When the grade comes back as less than perfect, the parents would act like it is not a big deal and remind the child that the grade would have been worse had they not done their part. They would also tell their child that when you are part of a team you both win together and lose together. That is what would be most helpful. If you think ahead, you will recognize that this group learning or children's team sports situation is exactly the same as working for a company or living together as a family. People who are grateful for the good attributes of others and who avoid blaming will naturally get along better, be more productive and help others to do the same. Science shows this to be true for both children and adults. Adults who choose to help workmates instead of just sticking to doing their own work end up being more successful in their careers, getting more promotions and improving the overall productivity of their workplace (Youngduk, Berry & Gonzalez-Mule, 2019).

Gratitude also enhances your child's ability to be persistent when things are difficult (Williams & Bartlett, 2014). One of the difficult things you have likely encountered with your anxious child is their tendency to want to give up when they get anxious. One of the main goals of good therapy is to teach your child that anxiety is a cue for stepping forward into the anxiety and staying on course, regardless of anxious thoughts or feelings. They have to learn to ignore the anxious impulse to freeze, avoid or fight and instead see the advantage of doing the thing they fear. Well-developed gratitude can be a powerful motivator when anxiety gets triggered. What would happen if your child felt grateful for the fact that exposure practice could get them better? When I encounter a child or teen who is grateful for finally finding someone who understands their anxiety and knows how to help them, especially after they have experienced treatment failure, the path to recovery is much smoother and rapid. I love it when these kids take a "Show me what to do no matter how difficult. I just want to get over my fear" attitude. It makes treatment a mutual effort to overcome their disorder rather than a fight to show them how much they stand to gain if only they would try some exposure practice.

My oldest son gave me a lesson in the power of gratitude that had a profound effect. Since my children were old enough to say grace (a prayer thanking God for the privilege of having food) before dinners, I had been trying to role model and promote gratitude. Part of our family's grace is to have everyone share something that happened or that they experienced that day that made them feel grateful. Sometimes they were good sports about this part of grace and other times it was like pulling teeth. I had the advantage, however, in forcing thoughts about gratitude, since no one was allowed to eat until grace had been successfully completed. When my kids gave me their adolescent version of "I dare you to make me be grateful!" response, I wondered if my attempt to insist on practicing gratitude was having any good effect.

Occasionally I worried that someday in their adult future they would be in a therapist's office complaining about being victimized by my attempts at good mental health. I imagined a shocked therapist saying something like "Oh my! That's emotional abuse, forcing you to be grateful when you were having a bad day. How on earth did you survive?!"

When my oldest was eleven he had been very ill with cyclic vomiting syndrome. The only treatment that would stop the frequent projectile vomiting was to go to the Emergency Department at a hospital an hour away to get a special intra-venous solution that stopped the vomiting, nausea, belly pain and head pain. Since the drive was long, he usually arrived severely dehydrated. One time he was so dehydrated that no one could insert the needle for the intravenous medicines. Multiple doctors and nurses repeatedly poked him with needles, trying to insert the needle without success. My son retched, winced and vomited throughout this ordeal while I watched with teary eyes. I felt extremely sorry for my son and for myself because we were yet again in the Emergency Department in this awful nightmarish situation. Eventually, the pediatric nurse who specialized in tiny babies was called for and after several attempts, she got the needle inserted. After the staff set up the medicine to drip into my son's veins, they left the room. I expected my son to start sobbing and complaining about how unfair his life was and about how everything bad happened to him. That was certainly what was going through my mind. Instead, he looked at me and said, "Mom, aren't you glad they finally got the needle in so I can now have a chance to stop throwing up?" His gratitude shamed me and made me realize that I was indeed grateful that he would soon feel better. He made me realize how lucky we both were that we lived near a city that had doctors who even knew what cyclic vomiting syndrome was and how to treat it. I knew that it could have been much worse.

Where is your gratitude about your child's situation and about your situation as the parent of a child with an anxiety disorder? Are you feeling sorry for your child, or for yourself as the parent who has to watch their child suffer? Do you see the blessing in being able to live in a world in which there is so much that can be done to help your child? Do you see the blessing in being able to read this book? Or do you see the blessing in having a child whose anxiety forces you to accept and enjoy their humanity without the illusion of them being some imagined version of perfect? There is also the blessing of what can happen to your child's character because of what they must learn in order to overcome their anxiety. Your ability to learn to be grateful in all situations is what will shape your child's ability to experience gratitude. More than any other recommendation in this book, the one to improve your own ability to experience deep gratitude in the struggle to raise your anxious child is the one that most matters to your family's well-being. If you master it, you will pave the way to implementing each of the other recommendations more effectively. You will rid yourself of the self-pity, resentment and false pity for your child that interferes with successful treatment. Both your and your child's mental health depends on it. If you are the type of parent who is reading this book, then I know that you are also likely to be the type of parent who wants to do their homework. So please pay attention to the suggestions I make later on for developing an attitude of gratitude in your home.

PARENT RESILIENCY RULE 13
Learn to be deeply grateful for your child's anxiety and for

all the circumstances of your life. Be grateful for all the
opportunities anxiety offers your child for their growth
and good character.

Deprivation and gratitude

What happens when you have everything you need? You take
it for granted. No matter how much someone explains to you
how lucky you are to live in a nice house, have a smartphone
with unlimited texting minutes or have new clothing that
you like, you cannot help but take it for granted because it
has always been that way. You can feel entitled to have all
the good and comfortable things because it has always been
there and therefore must be the way things should go in your
life. The aforementioned self-serving bias also dictates that,
if you are privileged, you will accidentally take credit for all
that is good in your life unless something happens to disabuse
you of this idea.

When we give too much out of love, or when we are
blessed with material wealth or access to comfortable, fun
things and activities, we begin to assume that this is just the
way life ought to be and we overlook how these things and
privileges came to be in our life. This happens to our children,
even when we do not intend for this to happen. When we
shower our children and teens with material goods that they
did not earn and shower them with access to special activities, tutors and more, then we accidentally create a world that
makes it seem easy and necessary to seek material goods and
to feel disgruntled when they are not readily available. We
also create a vacuum for gratitude and open the door for the
misperception of entitlement. I see this almost every day in
my work with families.

It is not unusual for me to hear parents tell me they are afraid to start treatment because their child has been rude, yells, hits or kicks, threatens to kill themselves or to run away when a parent or grandparent stops accommodating their anxiety and alternatively suggests that the child might have to earn access to toys, playdates, sports or digital devices by being better behaved and cooperating with treatment. When I bring up the idea of having a timeout from digital devices unless home practice for treatment and homework for school have been completed, I often hear this from the parents: "That is their phone/laptop/ipad/videogame console/special toy. I can't take that away!" Then the kid echoes this idea of entitlement, "You can't take away my stuff! It belongs to me!" Since I have yet to have a kid who has earned their own money to pay for all of their toys and digital devices, and also pay for their Internet access and texting/Internet surfing time, or who also contributes to paying the electrical bill for the home, I then ask, "Can you tell me who pays for the phone, the Internet account, the texting package on your phone account, the access to music files and movie files and who pays for the electricity in the house that powers your devices, or even provides a house that has electricity?" Most kids usually look at me mystified and answer that their parents are the ones who fund the things they love to use, but still do not catch on to the idea that they are receiving a privilege. The parents, however, quickly pick up this idea and then often begin to complain how they never had all these luxuries growing up and how their child is so lucky to have so much and how appalled they are by their kid's lack of appreciation for these wonderful things. They fail to see the disconnect between feeling entitled and having too much without having to earn access to these privileges.

The other problem you encounter as a human being is that your brain gets used to anything and everything. Just like you can get used to anxiety, you can get used to luxury, privilege and favorite foods. This is why pursuit of material wealth does not achieve great satisfaction in life. You get used to the next better thing, the next more luxurious thing and then you need to find something novel and more intense to register a new level of satisfaction in your brain. It's why you can redecorate your home and then forget to notice it after several months and eventually get bored with it and want to redecorate several years later when the fashions change. This means that after your child gets used to their new amazing toy, smartphone or iPad, that they swore they would be grateful to you for forever, they forget about the privilege of that special thing and take it for granted. On the other hand, if they have to repeatedly do something that costs them time, effort, money or inconvenience to maintain that special thing, it remains special because it is not guaranteed, might not always be available and might even go away. Think about it. Every time you see your bank balance decrease when you pay your rent or mortgage, you feel what it means to be able to afford your home and everything that you did to create that home. You also feel what it would be like were you to lose the income that makes your home possible and you feel grateful to be able to live in that home. The same thing happens when you have to choose between purchasing several things that you want. You have to plan, save and prioritize how you will spend your money and the thing that you planned, waited for and got to enjoy feels all that more special because it was not just handed to you as a gift. It also makes you very grateful when you have the rare experience of someone else's generosity that makes a special experience available, such as a friend inviting you to stay at their vacation home, or a boss who pays for a very expensive meal because you know that you could not make that happen through your own efforts. If you are used to paying the price of your living, then you become very grateful when blessed with a gift.

When I volunteered in Bhutan, I had the opportunity to work with some children who were raised in circumstances that required them to forgo education because they were needed to herd cattle in the mountains. They would have a half day's walk from the village to get to the pastures that housed their cattle. Their families were unable to provide books, toys or anything other than a few clothes and a daily meal. There was no indoor plumbing, no electricity and no special anything. When I would ask these children what they would like to earn as a reward for doing their exposure practice with their parents, they would tell me things like this: "I want to play the game with the rocks that my friends play. I want to play it with my parents." I asked what this game was, and they described a popular game that involved throwing small pebbles in a pebble version of bocce ball. They would also tell me, "I would like to sing with my parents, or have them tell me a story." One girl told me that she wanted to draw pictures with her mother. When I asked about this, she let me know that she had a favorite patch of dirt that she liked to use for drawing pictures with sticks. She just wanted to have guaranteed time away from tending the cattle so she could draw and have her mother admire her work. Teens would say similar things. They wanted to have time to just sit and enjoy their parents without having to do chores or work. I only had one teen, whose family was relatively wealthy, ask to earn access to a favorite video game. No one, including those whose families had wealth and were educated, however, asked to be able to earn something that could be purchased or that came from a store. They knew what it was to live in a country where there are few material goods to be bought and in which hard work was something that everyone had to do, including children. Many children and teens in Bhutan knew that if they were not working hard on the farm, then they were going to work very hard at school and household chores so they could avoid working very hard on the farm. They had a palpable sense of gratitude for the privilege of taking time off and of spending time with family and friends because they knew it was precious and not always guaranteed. This is in stark contrast to what I experience at work in a large urban and suburban area.

Do you see how this applies to your child? It means that you need to set up some strategic deprivation, so your child has the experience of knowing the difference between being comfortable, being privileged and doing without. This is the beauty of timeouts that behaviorists often fail to mention. When you lose access to something you enjoy, you begin to realize how precious it is and what a delight it is to have that privilege.

The problem for many of us, as parents, is that we over-focus upon creating comfort and being generous because that is how our relationship began with our child when they were an infant. It feels absolutely marvelous to be the parent who can give everything to an infant and see them smile, laugh or look adorable simply because we were generous. We forget that what is necessary for an infant is very different from what toddlers through emerging adults need. We get stuck in that place of wanting to see that gorgeous smile, that raucous laugh or that reaction of delight that made us so intoxicated when our child was an infant. We do not have to create poverty to help our children discriminate the difference between privilege and deprivation, but we do need to structure their lives so they can learn to appreciate that which we are able to provide. This means being willing to require effort to earn special items and avoiding giving so many gifts that your child is glutted and unable to savor the bounty. It means making them earn access to special items or activities contingent upon good behavior no matter what.

How to practice gratitude in your home

Savoring is an important part of practicing gratitude. Just writing a long list of single word items or rapidly rushing through a list of stock phrases, "Thank you God for my life and my daily meal," does not work. It is best if you focus upon things that happened that day and attempt to describe them in some detail. Research shows that the more you savor the better it works (Pitts, 2018). Thus, writing down a description of what happened, how you felt and why you felt that way works better than just writing down a one- or two-word representation of the moment. Writing works better than keyboarding, possibly because you have more time to savor the experience. If you are keeping a diary or a journal, stick to things that happened in the last 24 hours and force yourself, or your child, to find three things, whether it was a good day or an upsetting day. Sharing experiences aloud, in which you explain them to others, accomplishes the same benefit. Saving your lists of gratitude allows you to go back and re-read experiences to savor and inspire you when you are feeling low. I have years of saved journals and I enjoy re-reading them when I have a rough day or feel low in motivation. Initially, it helps to practice gratitude every day for the first month to help create the habit. After that point, it helps to do it about three times per week, so it does not become a chore. Lastly, sharing gratitude with others inspires them to experience gratitude, so be sure to let your family know about your moments of gratitude. Focusing upon the little daily things teaches people to notice and appreciate the wonder and blessing of being alive.

If your child suffers from entitlement directed toward all of their possessions, clothing, hobbies, etc., then try a little strategic poverty to help them recalibrate their sense of privilege. Confiscate the fancy clothes, smartphones, electronics and do a simulated poverty exercise in which they have a tight budget to shop with and wear thrift store clothing, eat pantry-type food, cook their own meal, use the local library for access to a computer and use public transportation instead of being conveniently transported. Have them pick up cardboard boxes to make a homeless-type shelter and sleep in the back garden, garage or a nearby field in their clothes and coat for a night to discover how wonderful their bed and bedding are. If you have always had easy access to special things, then they are no longer special. The same thing can be accomplished by having your child go on camping trips and volunteer service trips that provide meager accommodations, meager food and no access to the Internet. Ask them to think about what it is like for all of the children who do not have access to the privileges they enjoy. I did this exercise with my church's youth group and it was very effective in helping a group of privileged boys understand the nature of their privilege and the things they had taken for granted.

Even if you have ample money, consider paring down your purchases for your children and make them earn an allowance in order to pay for toys, special toiletries, clothing, school supplies or other necessary items so they learn the value of money and how to prioritize their spending. Make them get jobs and have chores even when you have house help, so they learn to care for themselves and appreciate the luxury of having others keep their lives neat. Give them a budget for purchasing new items for hobbies, sports or arts so they have to make forced choices based upon their priorities instead of getting everything they want.

Your child's gratitude about you and what you do

Many parents I see are hurt because their child does not appreciate their hard efforts and sacrifices made for the sake of the child. Perhaps you have felt this way, or perhaps you have felt let down by your child's lack of acknowledgment of all that you do. The truth is that children take their parents for granted, just like they do everything else. They are also immature and cannot possibly have the advantage of years of experience and acquired wisdom that accompany adulthood. For example, when you give a six-year-old the option of having three wishes, they usually will ask for unlimited toys and sweets. When you ask a twelve-year-old the same question, they will usually ask for large amounts of money or power. When you ask an eighteen-year-old, they will usually request the ability to influence the world order by eliminating war or famine along with something that they believe would give them great pleasure, such as unlimited opportunities to skateboard, or to get into their favorite university. Ask a parent the same question and you get a very different answer that would include the health and happiness of their children in addition to good things for mankind and some self-indulgences. Each of these different answers reflects developmental differences in maturity and ability, or lack of ability, to foresee the greater good.

> ### HOT TIP
>
> Do not expect your kids to express gratitude about your parenting until they are full-grown adults or become parents themselves.

So this means that you need to reset your expectations for your child's expression of gratitude to be realistic for their age and stage of psychological development. Their version of gratitude for who you are and what you do will reflect their view. For example, when my children were young their schools would always have a time for children to bring in parents who would talk about the type of job they did. Other parents in my son's school would bring in their battle gear from the Middle East (a dad who was a soldier), their dump truck (a driver for the nearby waste management facility), a baby calf and chickens (farmers), a stethoscope and x-rays of broken bones (a physician or nurse) and fire-fighting equipment (a firefighter). My son would always ask me to stay home and skip my turn to showcase my career because "All you do is help scared kids and that is boring!" Me attempting to explain the value of a PhD, job security and an income that paid for his private school was pointless because he was only eight. From his point of view, me coming in to read a story about a worried bunny who faced his fears was indeed boring. I would have to agree with him if I looked at my career from his eight-year-old point of view. What I did was boring.

The only time my career ever became interesting to my kids was when I was on television for Animal Planet's show on animal hoarding. Once again, my children's reaction was nothing that expressed any appreciation for what I was doing as part of the show. Whenever I overheard them talking about me being on the show, it had nothing to do with my intervention or professional skill. They would say things like "You have got to see how many dogs were in this lady's house on this TV show. My mom got to see it and she had to walk through all of the dog poop and pee and she had to act like she didn't get grossed out by it. She even got to see dead cats!" So, take the idea of getting a lot of gratitude from your child about all the sacrifices, hard work and agony you go through and try to forget about it for the next thirty years. Consider your child's gratitude for you to be a long-term project that is under construction and unlikely to yield a lot of satisfying results until they reach full adulthood and have the capacity to reflect upon what led to their success as a human being.

EXERCISES TO CULTIVATE GRATITUDE

1. Start a family gratitude journal and place it where every-one spends time and has time to write, such as the bathroom, the car or dining table. Encourage everyone to write their gratitude down and to read what others have written. I have found this to work really well with preteens and teens who can get prickly about being vulnerable face to face. It has often surprised parents with the sensitivity of their otherwise seemingly diffi-cult child.

2. Start a couple's gratitude journal with your partner that you keep in your bathroom or bedroom. This will help you develop a deep appreciation for what moves your partner and improve your ability to love each other because you know what matters to each other. You will be surprised by each other's gratitude and this keeps life in your relationship.

3. Start a daily time in which family members share aloud what they are grateful for from that day. Family meal-times, bedtime or commuting time in which you are all together in the car are the best times to do this. You can incorporate this into the family prayer at dinner or bedtime if that is your custom. Do not let people get away with a stock repeat answer. Make them refer to something specific and ask helpful open-ended ques-tions to get them thinking: "I know you think today was awful, but there must be at least one thing that was slightly less than terrible. What about what you ate

for a snack? The car not breaking down when I picked you up to go to practice? The dog being glad to see you when you walked into the house?"

4. Invite visitors to your family meals or commute to join your tradition of gratitude. People who visit my house share their gratitude at meals just like me, my husband and the children. This is a feel-good exercise that might feel a bit intimate at first but tends to bring about more closeness and shared good feelings.

5. Say aloud your spontaneous gratitude at the moment it occurs. When you are with your kids and notice a beautiful sunset, or hear a song you enjoy, say it and say how glad you are that you got to see it or hear it. Try to make this a habit, especially when things are difficult. For example, when you are stuck in slow traffic with your family in the car, say "Thank goodness the radio works and we can listen to something instead of just having to wait." When the doctor is running late, "I am so glad that at least we got in and can see the doctor. If would be so hard if we lived somewhere that did not have doctors."

6. Have your child write thank-you notes to teachers, coaches and tutors at the end of the year or season. Have your child describe what the adult did, and how they were helped and what they learned from this person. Better yet, get your child to read this note aloud to the person, or digitally record the message and send it to the person.

7. For yourself, think of one adult from your past who has been a positive influence in your life. Write a detailed thank-you note to them describing what they did, how it made you feel, what you learned and how you benefit from their influence today. Then read aloud this thank you to that person either in person, by videoconference or over the telephone.

8. Write down all the things that you can be grateful for since you realized your child had an anxiety disorder. Think about what has happened, who has been helpful, who you have met, what you and your child have learned about yourselves, other people and the goodness of kind people. Think about the experiences that you would have missed had your child not had an anxiety disorder. Think about what you now understand that you would never have learned had your child not had an anxiety disorder. Keep updating this list as your child continues their adventure in recovery.

9. Create strategic deprivation for your child to experience. You can get creative with this by declaring a no digital devices week for everyone in the family or having to select only three toys to play with for the entire week. You can show them how to do the laundry and make their own meals and have them become the cook who prepares everyone's meals for a weekend. The idea is to remove some of the things that are convenient, comfortable or taken for granted and to make your child do without or expend the effort to ensure the activity or event, such as supper, happens.

10. Refuse to help your child with chores or schoolwork of any kind so they learn to be grateful for help when it is required. Your child will learn to be more self-sufficient and resourceful in solving problems when they are required to do their own schoolwork and chores. If your child is rude, demanding or insulting about your help, immediately stop helping and walk away without coming back. Explain that your assistance is a privilege. Your child needs to learn that they are not entitled to your help at their own whim. They need to learn to be polite, respectful of your time and grateful for your help when you offer it.

CHAPTER 9

Love Is Gritty

Anxious children and teens need us to step up to the task of parenting them. Their struggle is with a particularly tricky foe. The foe of anxiety can narrow a child's thinking into a worried, negative, catastrophic, doubt-filled soup of ideas and images that has the capacity to stunt dreams, curtail choices and eliminate opportunities. Your child needs an adult who can demonstrate courage, calm and wisdom in the middle of struggle and fear. They need an adult who sees the big picture beyond the moment of fear and who understands how important it is to face anxiety and learn from it. They also need a parent who shows them how to enjoy life and savor the daily blessings that are there, if only they have the humility and grace to notice. In short, they need to learn to be well in the middle of suffering and to never take good moments for granted. How does this sound to you? Are you up to this challenge so you can be a good example and coach your child in what it means to be human, anxious and on the adventure of living with gusto in an uncertain world?

I hope that the previous chapters have inspired you to think deeply about what it means to be human, what it means to be a parent and what it means to embrace uncertainty and the inevitable daily risk of being human. Your perspective on your child's suffering with an anxiety disorder is very important. It colors the choices you make about how you speak, act and intervene when they struggle to manage their fear. If you accidentally pick the perspective that promotes over-parenting and over-accommodation, then you work at cross purposes with your goal for your child's good mental health. *Helicopter parenting* is the tendency to hover around your child, worry and intervene too much and too often. *Snowplow parenting* includes all the problems of helicopter parenting plus attempting to clear away all potential obstacles. Both are terrible choices that are common in our culture and reflect the past thirty years of pressure on parents to prevent all risk and accidentally discourage their children from becoming progressively more independent and self-correcting with each year of development. It has become common for legal punishments to be handed out to parents who leave their children alone in public places, for allowing children to walk to the playground alone or for failing to pick up children at the end of the school day. This is a sad outcome. Parents have become afraid to do the things they instinctively know are reasonable risks in child rearing. Many parents have become afraid of encouraging self-reliance for fear of attracting public shame or of being misperceived as neglectful. Many parents have accidentally begun to assume that life is very dangerous and therefore do not feel able to give their children the grace to learn without the immediate assistance of an adult.

I experienced this pressure some years ago when on a winter day I went to pick up my oldest son's new special shoes made to fit his foot and ankle braces. My youngest son was an infant who had been up all night with a strep infection. I had been waiting several months to get medical authorization for new foot and ankle braces which meant that my oldest son was wearing braces that he had outgrown and that required me to cut out the toes of his shoes to accommodate his growing feet. Once his braces arrived, we had to take them to a special shoe store to get the braces measured and new shoes ordered that were made to handle foot and ankle braces. Then we had to wait two weeks to receive the shoes. My son had to wear the ill-fitting shoes with toes cut out in the meantime, which made me feel like a bad mom even though I could do nothing to change the situation. The cost for the braces was so prohibitive that my husband and I needed to make sure their cost was covered by insurance. So, when I got the call from the shoe store, I gathered up both kids and dashed to the shoe store. While on the way to the shoe store, my infant son who had just come down with strep finally fell asleep for the first time in 24 hours. I decided that I would not disturb him so he could continue sleeping in the car. I locked him in the car and went inside the store where it took about twenty minutes to get his brother's shoes, try them on and adjust them so everything fit together. I ran out to the car every five minutes to verify that my youngest was still asleep and then would dash back into the store. The main reason I ran out to the car was to prove to any bystanders that I was making sure my infant son was not in distress. Had I felt brave enough, I would have just left him sleeping since I knew he was exhausted and comfortable enough to sleep.

When we finally left the store, I saw a woman standing by my car, peering in at my sleeping son and dialing a number on her mobile phone. I ran up and asked her what was going on. She yelled at me, telling me that I had abandoned my child and was breaking the law and that she was calling the police to protect my son. I wish I could say that I was polite in how I handled this situation, but I had lost too much sleep and I lost my temper. I yelled at her and told her that she had no idea what was going on and that the sleeping child had strep and had not slept in the past 24 hours and that his brother had been waiting for his new shoes and that she better mind her own business and go ahead and call the cops if she really believed that I was an abuser. Only I didn't say it quite as nicely as that and I drove off in a huff.

What scared me and still angers me is that this woman assumed that this was a dangerous situation without any evidence of apparent danger or neglect. She became self-righteous about what should be done and responded to the cultural hype about child neglect and child abuse. She likely was a mother and grandmother who knew what it was like to raise children and deal with the repeating chaos of parenting. She had lost her empathy, her sympathy and her ability to sensibly think about a situation in which nothing bad was happening. Her response was one that I had feared and that I knew made many parents cave in to the pressure to be overprotective or over accommodating.

I have also been in many public places implementing a timeout for my children or the children I treat and been dismayed when someone expresses disapproval and clucks about the sight of a crying, yelling or angry and anxious child. Do they really believe that a successful parent or therapist could so skillfully manage a child or teen's life so that no one gets upset or no tantrums occurs in a public place? Do they really expect that all children and teens should be convenient, have no problems that cause public or private disruption, or that make the moment inconvenient for others? One thing is clear, they have lost their sense of humor and a healthy understanding that no parent, therapist, child or teen is perfect. They have also misperceived danger and risk and recast the role of parent as preventer of all distress, risk, harm and public annoyance. No parent can accomplish these things. Attempting to eliminate risk and suffering only backfires into raising a child who is surprised and undone by the stress of normal living and the frustration of ordinary human problems, such as having an anxiety disorder.

You need to embrace the conflict and chaos that is inherent in parenting and call it for what it is, normal. Having raised children and worked with children for many years, I cannot imagine how one could possibly shepherd an infant to adulthood without some crazy blips upon the way. If a quarter of the world population experiences full-fledged anxiety disorders and a similar percentage experiences other mental health disorders, then addressing mental health problems is going to be part of child rearing for at least half of the population. One out of every four parents will see symptoms of anxiety in their child that requires their attention. When you set the stage for mental wellness, you set the stage for your child to flourish regardless of their anxiety disorder. This is exciting! You really can have fun and teach your child to have fun despite the presence of their symptoms. You can show them how to approach their fears with gusto and determination to live life as though it is an adventure instead of feeling victimized and fragile.

HOT TIP

It takes courage and a good sense of humor to raise anxious kids who can become mentally healthy, joyful resilient adults. Be the parent who is willing to be different and up to the job!

The other bold stance you need to take is to believe that it is possible for your child to develop great mental wellness *and* have an anxiety disorder at the same time. Having an anxiety disorder is not an automatic prescription for poor mental health. It is, however, an automatic opportunity for learning to become a risk taker, learning to persevere when you feel like giving up and learning to believe in a better self that does not have to be limited by anxiety or trying to always play it safe. Kids who learn to overcome anxiety and do things despite feeling scared are prepared to handle the complicated and anxiety-provoking situations that all adults face. It is much easier to succeed as an adult when you are not afraid of getting anxious and know that you can do difficult things in order to make good things happen. Adults need to stay calm when others are losing their temper. Adults need to be willing to do many things that take them outside their comfort zone and they need to be willing to take big risks for the sake of attaining their goals. Adults need to go to job interviews and ask for raises despite feeling anxious. They need to do many things that predictably provoke anxiety without giving up. Think what would have happened to mankind had people not been willing to migrate across mountains and oceans to find a better life even though they knew the journey was perilous. What would have happened if no one was willing to go into battle for the sake of a better life and freedom from tyranny? The people who climbed the tallest mountains or dared to think new thoughts and acted upon them were the ones who were gritty and willing to try new and difficult things even though they were scared. These adventurers inspire all of us to dream bigger and to try new things that lead to new inventions, new paradigms and things that can make life better for everyone. This kind of resilience also gives us strength to be self-controlled and able to build community when life is very difficult. It takes great strength of character to be the adult who can be gentle when they are scared, to be kind when they are in crisis or to be loyal when they are angry or disappointed. Your child needs you to believe in their ability to become this kind of person and to show them how to use their experience of overcoming anxiety to their best advantage.

The way you view your child's anxiety disorder will influence the way you approach the task of parenting. Be willing to ask yourself whether you are you trying to make your child comfortable at the expense of their future or are you willing to deliberately make your child uncomfortable, so they are prepared for their future? Your willingness to become a role model of courageous risk taking in your role of parent is critical to your ability to be helpful in the process of parenting an anxious child. You will need to learn to ignore your own worry about what might go wrong and instead refocus upon all that your child stands to gain from learning the skills mentioned in this book. Hopefully you can see that recovery involves much more than just doing all of the right exposure therapy assignments and taking the right medications. It involves a mindset change and acquisition of the following vital skills that promote good mental wellness.

1. Accept suffering as a normal part of being human, even for children.

2. Let go of the fantasy of the perfect child, the perfect childhood or the idea that "the best" of anything will guarantee a happy life for your child.

3. Learn to enjoy every good moment, including the ones

that occur in the midst of suffering, and embrace the messy hilarity of parenting.

4. Adopt a compassionate view toward yourself, your child and for those who deal with your child.

5. Realize the value of struggle and renounce perfectionism in your home.

6. Cultivate good humor and learn to find the funny in your child's anxiety and their recovery. Help them to do the same.

7. Accept uncertainty and recognize that there is no such thing as guaranteeing the future. Embrace risk taking for yourself and your child as a means toward full zesty living.

8. Make gratitude your default setting for life. Be willing to teach your child to be grateful through helping them take perspective and making them experience some therapeutic deprivation.

9. Get gritty with your love for your child so they can acquire grit and resilience.

If you acquire these skills, then you will discover that the process of raising your anxious child can be fun even though it has challenges and frustration built into the process. You will be able to enjoy the strengths of your child while not getting overly upset about their need for growth in their areas of vulnerability. Your ability to acquire a calm purposeful approach to their anxiety will make it easier for them to do the same. Your willingness to assume that your child's anxiety is an opportunity for developing character and necessary skills for successful adulthood will transform your false sense of tragedy or guilt into joyful purpose. You will also be able to learn to laugh at the messy hilarity of parenting an anxious child when you appreciate the ironic absurdity that children need life's challenges in order to hone skills in mental wellness. Your deep belly laughs will signal to your child and family that nothing terrible is happening and that being human is quite often absurd, even when it is frustrating. You will also acquire peace of mind about being the parent who cannot be perfect and who cannot raise a perfect child. This will remove the terrible pressure to turn your child's life into a recovery project instead of an opportunity for improved mental wellness. The parents I have seen take this journey discover great joy, clarity of purpose and good humor about all the things that once felt overwhelming about being the parent of an anxious child. They learn that privilege cannot confer these priceless skills and that the best way to handle anxiety is to face it head on with gusto. They learn that suffering offers great opportunity when you realize the value of learning to overcome things that may feel unfair and painful. I know that you, too, can turn your child's journey through anxiety into an adventure into mental wellness. If you do, you will bless your child by getting off the hamster wheel of perfectionism and overparenting. You will instead lead them on the adventure of living each day with zest, humility and courage to face whatever might come their way. May you and your family be blessed on this journey!

References

Achor, S. (2010) *The Happiness Advantage: How a Positive Brain Fuels Success in Life.* New York: Currency.

Algoe, S., Gable, S. & Maisel, N. (2010) 'It's the little things: Everyday gratitude as a booster shot for romantic relationships.' *Personal Relationships 17,* 2, 217–233.

Allen, A., Barton, J. & Stevenson, O. (2015) 'Presenting a self-compassionate image after an interpersonal transgression.' *Self and Identity 14,* 33–50.

American Psychological Association (APA). (2012) 'Growing up grateful gives teens multiple mental health benefits.' *Science-Daily* August 6. Accessed on 1/7/2021 at www.sciencedaily.com/releases/2012/08/120806093938.htm.

Auerbach R., Mortier P., Bruffaerts, R., Alonso, J., *et al.* (2018) 'WHO world mental health surveys international college student project: Prevalence and distribution of mental disorders.' *Journal of Abnormal Psychology 127,* 623–638.

Australian Government Department of Health (2009) *The Mental Health of Australians 2: Prevalence of Mental Disorders in the Australian Population.* Accessed on 1/28/2021 at www1.health.gov.au/internet/publications/publishing.nsf/Content/mental-pubs-m-mhaust2-toc~mental-pubs-m-mhaust2-hig~mental-pubs-m-mhaust2-hig-pre#:~:text=The%20prevalence%20of%20mental%20disorders%20is%20the%20proportion,at%20some%20point%20in%20their%20lifetime%20%28figure%201%29.

Bains, G., Berk, L., Daher, N., Lohman, E., *et al.* (2014) 'The effect of humor on short-term memory in older adults: A new component for whole-person wellness.' *Advances in Mind-body Medicine 28*, 2, 16–24.

Berger, N., Holmes, K., Gore, J., Gore, J. & Archer, J. (2019) 'Charting career aspirations: A latent class mixture model of aspiration trajectories in childhood and adolescence.' *Australian Educational Research 47*, 651–678.

Borchard, T. (2018) '6 benefits of roughhousing.' *PsychCentral.* Accessed on 1/7/2021 at https://psychcentral.com/lib/6-benefits-of-roughhousing-for-kids.

Bourg-Carter, S. (2011) 'The natural high of laughter.' *Psychology Today*, November 22. Accessed on 1/8/2021 at www.psychologytoday.com/us/blog/high-octane-women/201111/the-natural-high-laughter.

Burton, N. (2020) 'The 7 real reasons for laughing.' *Psychology Today*, September 20. Accessed on 1/8/2021 at www.psychologytoday.com/us/blog/hide-and-seek/202009/the-7-real-reasons-laughing.

Busby, E. (2018) June 7. 'Fewer university students say they are happy and believe lives to be worthwhile, survey finds.' *Independent*, June 7. Accessed on 1/8/2021 at www.independent.co.uk/news/education/education-news/mental-health-students-wellbeing-universities-survey-suicides-a8386701.html.

Eckelkamp, S. (2014) 'Laughter therapy is the new meditation.' *Time*, May 2. Accessed on 1/8/2021 at https://time.com/84987/laughter-may-be-the-new-meditation.

Emmons, R. and McCullough, M. (2003) 'Counting blessings versus burdens: An experimental investigation of gratitude and subjective well-being in daily life.' *Journal of Personality and Social Psychology 84*, 2, 377–389.

Grcevich, S. (2016) 'Special needs and divorce: What does the data say?' *Key Ministry Blog*, March 28. Accessed on 1/8/2021 at www.keyministry.org/church4everychild/2016/3/28/special-needs-and-divorce-what-does-the-data-say.

Hardy, S. (2012) *Housewife: Marriage and Homemaking in the 1950s.* Stroud: The History Press.

Kelley, A. (2020) 'Changing America, 41 percent of US adults report mental illness due to pandemic stress.' *The Hill*, August 13. Accessed on 1/8/2021 at https://thehill.com/changing-america/well-being/mental-health/511870-41-percent-of-us-adults-report-mental-illness-due.

Keltner, D. & Marsh, J. (2015) 'How gratitude beats materialism.' *The Greater Good Magazine*, January 8. Accessed on 1/27/2021 at https://greatergood.berkeley.edu/article/item/materialism_gratitude_happiness.

Kim, M. (2016) 'Independent, risk taking teenagers may be better at learning, study finds.' *Independent*, February 24. Accessed on 1/8/2021 at www.independent.co.uk/news/science/risk-taking-teenagers-may-be-better-learning-study-finds-a6892651.html.

Leanos, S., Kürüm, E., Strickland-Hughes, C.M., Ditta, A.S., *et al.* (2019) 'The impact of learning multiple real-world skills on cognitive abilities and functional independence in healthy older adults.' *The Journals of Gerontology: Series B 75*, 6, 1155–1169.

Liu, Z., Riggio, R.E., Day, D.V., Zheng, C., Dai, S. & Bian, Y. (2019) 'Leader development begins at home: Overparenting harms adolescent leader emergence.' *Journal of Applied Psychology 104*, 10, 1226–1242.

McGonigal, K. (2015) *The Upside of Stress: Why Stress Is Good for You, and How to Get Good at It.* New York: Penguin Random House.

Marques de Miranda, D., da Silva Athanasio, B., Sena Oliveira, A.C. & Simoes-e-Silva, A.C. (2020) 'How is COVID-19 pandemic impacting mental health of children and adolescents?' *International Journal of Disaster Risk Reduction, 51*, art. 101845.

Murkoff, H. (2016) *What to Expect When You're Expecting*, 5th edition. New York: Workman Publishing.

Neff, K.D. (2012) 'The Science of Self-Compassion.' In C. Germer and R. Siegel (eds.) *Compassion and Wisdom in Psychotherapy.* New York: Guilford Press.

Neff, K.D., Long, P., Know, M., Davidson, O., *et al.* (2018) 'The forest and the trees: Examining the association of self-compassion and its positive and negative components with psychological functioning.' *Self and Identity 17*, 627–645.

Noone, P. (2017) 'The Holmes–Rahe Stress Inventory.' *Occupational Medicine (London) 67*, 581–582.

Pew Research Center. (2015) *Parenting in America. Numbers, Facts and Data Saving the World.* Accessed on 1/8/2021 at www.pewsocial-trends.org/2015/12/17/3-parenting-approaches-and-concerns.

Pitts, M.J. (2018) 'The language and social psychology of savoring: Advancing the communication savoring model.' *Journal of Language and Social Psychology 38,* 237.

Posner, M.I., Rothbart, M.K., Sheese, B.E. & Voelker, P. (2014) 'Developing attention: Behavioral and brain mechanisms.' *Advances in Neuroscience,* art. 405094.

Randolph, S. (2017) 'The power of gratitude.' *Workplace Health Safety 65,* 144.

Robinson, B. (2020) 'New study shows how perfection and anxiety can lead to helicopter parenting.' *Forbes,* October 3. Accessed on 1/8/2021 at www.forbes.com/sites/bryanrobinson/2020/10/03/new-study-shows-how-perfection-and-anxiety-can-lead-to-helicopter-parenting/?sh=f4f4a7b4f834.

Rodriguez, A. (2019) 'A 3-year-old died falling off an airport escalator. Now, his mom faces child abuse charges.' *USA Today,* Nov 21. Accessed on 1/8/2021 at www.usatoday.com/story/news/nation/2019/11/21/north-carolina-mom-charged-after-son-dies-airport-escalator/4257423002.

Scherer, N., Verhey, I. & Kuper, H. (2019) 'Depression and anxiety in parents of children with intellectual and developmental disabilities: A systematic review and meta-analysis.' *PLOS ONE 14,* 7, art. e0219888.

Schiffrin, H., Godfrey, H., Liss, M. & Erchull, M. (2015) 'Intensive parenting: Does it have the desired impact on child outcomes?' *Journal of Child and Family Studies 24,* 2322–2331.

SINTEF. (2015) 'Risk-takers are smarter, according to a new study.' *ScienceDaily.* Accessed on 1/28/2021 at www.sciencedaily.com/releases/2015/11/151130113545.htm.

Smith, M., Sherry, S., Chen, S., Saklofske, D., *et al.* (2018) 'The perniciousness of perfectionism: A meta-analytic review of the perfectionism-suicide relationship.' *Journal of Personality 86,* 522–542.

Steel, Z., Marnane, C., Iranpour, C., Chey, T., *et al.* (2014) 'The global prevalence of common mental disorders: A systematic review and meta-analysis 1980–2013.' *International Journal of Epidemiology 43*, 476–493.

Tala, A. (2019) 'Thanks for everything: A review on gratitude from neurobiology to clinic.' *Revista Medica de Chile 147*, 755–761.

Vorobyev, V., Kwon, M., Moe, D., Parkkola, R. & Hämäläinen, H. (2016) 'Risk-taking behavior in a computerized driving task: Brain activation correlates of decision-making, outcome, and peer influence in male adolescents.' *PLOS ONE 10*, art. 0129516.

Warren, R., Smeets, E. & Neff, K.D. (2016) 'Self-criticism and self-compassion: Risk and resilience for psychopathology.' *Current Psychiatry 15*, 18–32.

Williams, L.A. & Bartlett, M.Y. (2014) 'Warm thanks: Gratitude expression facilitates social affiliation in new relationships via perceived warmth.' *Emotion, 15*, 1.

Yim, J. (2016) 'Therapeutic benefits of laughter in mental health: A theoretical review.' *Tohoku Journal of Experimental Medicine 239*, 243–249.

Yoshimura, S. & Berzins, K. (2017) 'Grateful experiences and expressions: The role of gratitude expressions in the link between gratitude experiences and well-being.' *Review of Communication 17*, 106.

Youngduk, L., Berry, C. & Gonzalez-Mule, E. (2019) 'The importance of being humble: A meta-analysis and incremental validity analysis of the relationship between honesty-humility and job performance.' *Journal of Applied Psychology 104*, 1535–1546.

Zhengguang, L., Riggio, R., Day, D., Zhen, C., Dai, S. & Yufang, D. (2019) 'Leader development begins at home: Overparenting harms adolescent leader emergence.' *Journal of Applied Psychology 104*, 1226–1242.

Resources

Documentary: Chasing Childhood, www.chasingchildhooddoc. com.

This documentary can be purchased for screening for individuals, parent groups, community groups or other groups. It describes the science behind the dangers of overparenting and helps parents, educators and community members develop ideas for improving the mental wellness for any child or teen, especially those who have become anxious through accidental overparenting.

Dr Karen Cassiday, *Imperfect Fear: Why Parenting Doesn't Need a Handbook. TEDxYouth at Wonderland Road.* Accessed on 1/8/2021 at www.youtube.com/watch?v=c7OaAO4H_Pc.

TEDx talk of author telling how she discovered how to love and enjoy her disabled and socially anxious son in the middle of Walt Disney World.

Kelly McGonigal, *How to Make Stress Your Friend.* Accessed on 1/8/2021 at www.ted.com/talks/kelly_mcgonigal_how_to_ make_stress_your_friend?language=en.

TED talk explaining how attitudes about stress are the problem, not the experience of stress itself.

Israel Kalman, PhD, *Why Victims Are the Key to Ending Bullying*. Accessed on 1/8/2021 at www.youtube.com/watch?v= 6KH9L5gSE8c&feature=youtu.be.

Video about evidence-based ways to handle bullying.

Dacher Keltner & Jason Marsh, *How Gratitude Beats Materialism*. Accessed on 1/8/2021 at https://greatergood.berkeley.edu/ article/ITEM/materialism_gratitude_happiness.

Index

Other JKP books

Bettina Hohnen, Jane Gilmour & Tara Murphy
Foreword by Sarah-Jayne Blakemore
Illustrated by Douglas Broadley

The Incredible Teenage Brain
Everything You Need to Know
to Unlock Your Teen's Potential
*Bettina Hohnen, Jane Gilmour and
Tara Murphy*
Illustrated by Douglas Broadley
Foreword by Sarah Jayne Blakemore

£15.99 | $21.95 | PB | 360PP |
ISBN 978 1 78592 557 3 |
eISBN 978 1 78450 952 1

An accessible, expert guide to the incredible potential of
the teen brain from three psychologists. The authors give
practical tips and advice based on the very latest research that
reappraises the adolescent years as an exciting and unique
period of development, showing how we can best support
teens' emotional, social and intellectual development.

Bettina, Jane and Tara are clinical psychologists who have a
specialist interest in neuropsychology and are all based at or
have worked at Great Ormond Street Hospital and University
College London. All have academic backgrounds and over 20
years' experience working with children, young people and
families, and delivering training to parents and professionals.

Teen Mental Health in an Online World
Supporting Young People around their Use of Social Media, Apps, Gaming, Texting and the Rest
Victoria Betton and James Woollard

£16.99 | $24.95 | PB | 296PP |
ISBN 978 1 78592 468 2 |
eISBN 978 1 78450 852 4

This essential book shows practitioners how they can engage with teens' online lives to support their mental health. It looks at the positive effects online spaces have on mental health, as well as the risks such as bullying, sexting and addiction. It also provides a framework to help teens develop resilience in respect of their internet use.

Dr Victoria Betton is a well-known speaker on mental health, digital and social media. She runs mHabitat, an NHS hosted digital innovation organization, and researches and reports on digital for the NHS.

Dr James Woollard is a consultant child and adolescent psychiatrist at Oxleas NHS Foundation Trust and Senior Fellow in Mental Health Technology and Innovation at NHS England.

Starving the Anxiety Gremlin
A Cognitive Behavioural
Therapy Workbook on Anxiety
Management for Young People
Kate Collins-Donnelly

£12.99 | $19.95 | PB | 168PP |
ISBN 978 1 84905 341 9 |
eISBN 978 0 85700 673 8

This engaging workbook helps young people aged 10+ understand and manage anxiety. Based on cognitive behavioral therapy principles, the activities will help young people understand why they get anxious and how to use simple, practical techniques to manage and control their anxiety. Suitable to work through alone or with a parent or practitioner.

Kate Collins-Donnelly has worked as a therapist, psychologist, criminologist and anger management consultant based in the UK for many years. She presently runs a successful independent consultancy practice which provides cognitive behavioral therapy, counseling, coaching and training, and is head of the Psychological and Criminological Research Division. She is the author of *Starving the Anger Gremlin*, *Starving the Depression Gremlin* and *Starving the Stress Gremlin*.

My Anxiety Handbook
Getting Back on Track
Sue Knowles, Bridie Gallagher and Phoebe McEwen
Illustrated by Emmeline Pidgen

£12.99 | $19.95 | PB | 192PP |
ISBN 978 1 78592 440 8 |
eISBN 978 1 78450 813 5

An accessible, easy-to-use anxiety survival guide for young people aged 12–18. Co-authored by psychologists and a young person with anxiety, it looks at the causes of anxiety and offers tested methods and simple exercises to reduce the reader's anxious feelings. Includes chapters on sleep, exams and transitions.

Dr Sue Knowles is a senior clinical psychologist with longstanding experience of working with young people and their carers in a range of settings. She works for the psychological services organization Changing Minds UK [www.changingmindsuk.com].

Dr Bridie Gallagher is a senior clinical psychologist working with adolescents in acute inpatient environments and secure welfare accommodation. She also teaches on the Leeds and Lancaster clinical psychology doctorate courses.

Phoebe McEwen is a college student with lived experience of anxiety.